Staples+5

TANORRIA ASKEW

Publisher Mike Sanders
Senior Editor Ann Barton
Design Director William Thomas
Food Photography Martina Jackson
Food Stylist Lovoni Walker
Chef Ashley Brooks
Recipe Tester Diamond Alexander
Proofreaders Lisa Starnes, Monica Stone
Indexer Celia McCoy

First American Edition, 2021
Published in the United States by DK Publishing
6081 E. 82nd St., Indianapolis, IN 46250

21 22 23 24 25   10 9 8 7 6 5 4 3 2 1
001-325076-OCT2021

ISBN 978-0-7440-4215-3
Library of Congress Catalog Number: 2021930997

Note: This publication contains the opinions and ideas of its author. It is intended to provide helpful and informative material on the subject matter covered. It is sold with the understanding that the author and publisher are not engaged in rendering professional services in the book.
If the reader requires personal assistance or advice, a competent professional should be consulted. The author and publisher specifically disclaim any responsibility for any liability, loss, or risk, personal or otherwise, which is incurred as a consequence, directly or indirectly, of the use and application of any of the contents of this book.

Trademarks: All terms mentioned in this book that are known to be or are suspected of being trademarks or service marks have been appropriately capitalized. Alpha Books, DK, and Penguin Random House LLC cannot attest to the accuracy of this information. Use of a term in this book should not be regarded as affecting the validity of any trademark or service mark.

DK books are available at special discounts when purchased in bulk for sales promotions, premiums, fund-raising, or educational use.
For details, contact: SpecialSales@dk.com

Printed and bound in China

Cover image and pages 2, 6, 9, 10 © Leah Rife
Photo page 15 © Shutterstock
All other images © Dorling Kindersley Limited
For further information see: www.dkimages.com

For the curious
www.dk.com

Staples+5

*To all the brilliant, dynamic, incomparable
Black women who make something out of nothing.*

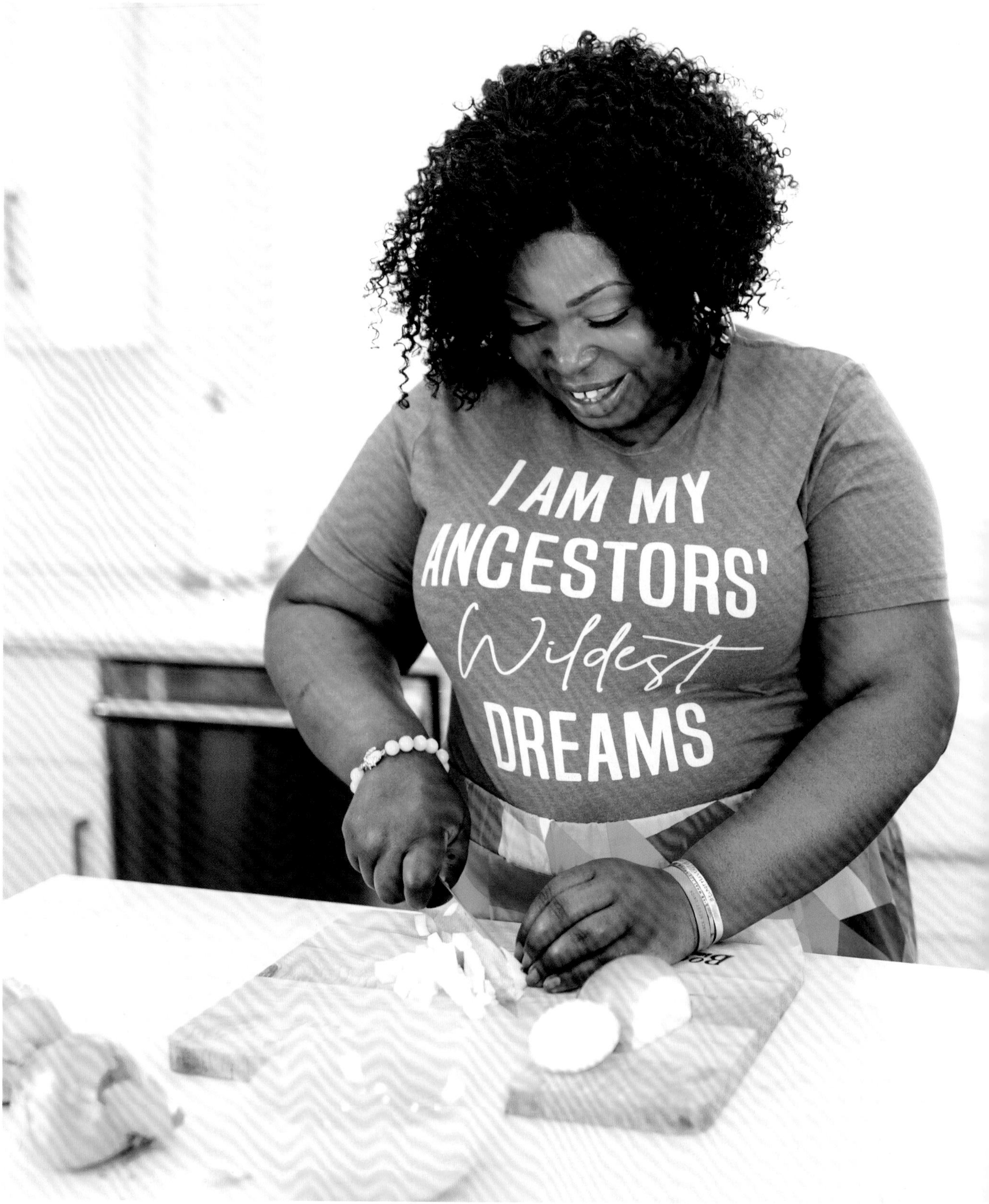
I AM MY
ANCESTORS'
Wildest
DREAMS

Contents

Introduction

I grew up in a Southern-bred household in the middle of the Midwest. Translation: My family was from the South, but we lived in Indiana because of my dad's job. We often celebrated holidays back home in Tennessee, where my extended family entertained and fed people. My cooking is influenced by the flavors of the South, where everything is made from scratch and cooked low and slow, as well as the comfort foods of the Midwest, known for its hearty meals of meat and potatoes.

I learned early on that my family had a gift for sharing meals with others. We had a large Sunday dinner at our house almost every week, and there was always someone following us home from church to share in that meal. Mom never knew about our Sunday dinner guests in advance because my dad was always extending last-minute invitations. He would meet a new face at church, get to talking, and the next thing we knew, they were at our dinner table.

Mom was left to make magic. Despite her frustration, she always pulled off an excellent meal and never seemed frazzled. She would pull out staple ingredients from her pantry and make enough for everyone to take home leftovers. My mom makes everything from scratch and full of flavor, and it is all because she relies on her pantry staples. It's how I learned to cook, and it's how I know to survive.

Once I got my first apartment, I understood the beauty of what food can do. It unites people. I could easily convince my friends to come over by describing what I was going to make. They always raved about my cooking abilities. Those same friends encouraged me to make a career out of feeding people. That is how I launched my personal chef service, Tanorria's Table. The ultimate validation of my career change came in 2016 when I auditioned for Season 7 of *MasterChef*, hosted by Gordon Ramsay. Making it to the show and winning a white apron changed my whole world. Hearing positive feedback from judges like Gordon Ramsay, Christina Tosi, and Aarón Sánchez solidified that I was doing the right thing. It amplified my desire to share my cooking with people.

Cooking is not only my career; it is also my gift. Transforming the most fundamental ingredients into something beautiful is the gift passed down to me from a lineage of Black women. There is a rich history in these recipes. Culture is celebrated in these recipes, and the magic of making something out of nothing is revealed. The use of seasoning and spices, along with the mission of making well-seasoned food, comes from my ancestors and has become my gift to you. It is sprinkled throughout this entire book. I hope you savor it.

The Staples +5 Philosophy

My Grandma Judy was a single mother of five. She knew better than anyone how to make something out of nothing, and she relied on pantry staples to feed her family daily. As a kid, my mom would always tell me, "If anything ever goes awry and you're low on money, you can do anything with a bag of rice and a bag of flour." She learned that from her mom, and Grandma Judy was right. This is the philosophy behind *Staples +5*.

STOCK YOUR PANTRY

A well-stocked pantry gives you a solid foundation on which to cook nourishing meals. The recipes in this book are all based on the *Staples* +5 Pantry List (page 12), which includes 35 essential ingredients. Review that list, and take inventory of what you have. Is your pantry bursting with items that are old or rarely used? Refresh your ingredients by throwing out anything that's expired. Buy fresh bags of flour and cornmeal. Grab a variety of canned and dried beans for those snowy days when "warm and cozy" is a requirement. Buy good quality butter in bulk and freeze it. Always, always, always have bacon on hand. Always. Keep your spice cabinet stocked and your bottles of oil and vinegar plentiful.

COOK FROM SCRATCH

Once you have your staples in place, you're ready to cook. All the recipes in this book rely on pantry staples plus up to five additional fresh ingredients. (Any ingredients beyond those on the staples list are marked with a ⊕ on the ingredients list.) Whenever possible, I like to cook from scratch. Whether we're talking about pie crust or pickles, I have always found that food is more affordable and tastes better when made from scratch. Instead of reaching for premade mixes, learn how to make the food you love, and keep those ingredients on hand.

CONQUER THE TECHNIQUES

So much of cooking is about mastering a basic technique and building on it. *Staples +5* is a map that you can use to make the most of your pantry. Read over each recipe to learn the method. Try out the flavor combinations I created and then create your own. You just might surprise yourself. We are not shooting for perfection here. We are shooting for tasty.

SHARE WHAT YOU MAKE

I recently tested a recipe and took the finished product to a friend who was struggling to juggle her kids and an ill partner. The ingredients in that dish were primarily staples from my pantry. She loved it, and I felt confident sharing the recipe with her, knowing that she could recreate it easily with staples from her own pantry. Let this book guide you through your pantry as you navigate what to make for a friend in need or when unexpected guests arrive. Use it as a resource for everything you can make in a time of crisis when grocery store shelves are sparsely stocked. Lean into these recipes when you are looking for a way to show love to others. Take advantage of the tips, tricks, and advice gifted throughout this book. I've tried it, failed at it, and tried it again so that you don't have to.

Be bold. Be fearless. Cook good food so that you can always enjoy good food.

The Staples +5 Pantry List

Every pantry should include these 35 ingredients. They are economical, practical, and versatile. These are the "staple" ingredients that form the basis of every recipe in this book. All recipes can be made with these ingredients plus up to five additional ingredients. (Additional ingredients are marked with a ⊕ in the recipes.)

BAKING

- ○ All-purpose flour
- ○ Cornmeal
- ○ Baking powder
- ○ Baking soda
- ○ Granulated sugar
- ○ Brown sugar (light or dark)
- ○ Cornstarch or arrowroot powder

CANS & CARTONS

- ○ Canned beans
- ○ Crushed tomatoes
- ○ Chicken stock

MEATS & DAIRY

- ○ Bacon
- ○ Parmesan cheese
- ○ Butter

OILS & VINEGARS

- ○ Canola oil or vegetable oil
- ○ Extra-virgin olive oil
- ○ Apple cider or red wine vinegar
- ○ Balsamic vinegar

PRODUCE

- ○ Onions
- ○ Russet potatoes
- ○ Sweet potatoes
- ○ Garlic

CONDIMENTS & SAUCES

- ○ Soy sauce
- ○ Worcestershire sauce
- ○ Honey
- ○ Mustard

RICE, BEANS, & PASTA

- ○ Rice
- ○ Dried beans
- ○ Dried pasta

SEASONINGS & SPICES

- ○ Kosher salt
- ○ Black pepper
- ○ Granulated garlic
- ○ Onion powder
- ○ Paprika (smoked or sweet)
- ○ Ground cinnamon
- ○ Bay leaves

INGREDIENT INFO

BAKING

All-purpose flour: Any all-purpose flour will do, but my go-to is White Lily flour. It is made from soft wheat, which has a lower protein content than other wheat varieties, making light and fluffy.) White Lily is not widely available outside of the southern United States; if you find it, stock up!

Cornmeal: Look for fine- or medium-ground yellow cornmeal. If you can get your hands on White Lily cornmeal, buy it in bulk.

CANS & CARTONS

Canned beans: If you have canned beans, you're not far from a meal. Kidney beans, pinto beans, navy beans, black-eyed peas, chickpeas, and black beans are all good choices. Most bean recipes can be adapted to use another bean variety if you don't have the one that's called for on hand.

Crushed tomatoes: Canned crushed tomatoes are more versatile than tomato sauce, and they add a body and texture that tomato sauce can't accomplish.

Chicken stock: There is a chicken stock recipe in this cookbook, but I tend to use it faster than I can make it and freeze it. There is no shame in store-bought chicken stock. Just make sure it's a high-quality brand without unnecessary additives.

MEATS & DAIRY

These refrigerated items are technically perishable, but they can last for weeks in the refrigerator or months in the freezer, making it easy to buy them in bulk and keep them on hand.

Bacon: Does bacon need an explanation? As a cured meat, bacon has a long shelf life, and it can be used in many applications to add robust, smoky flavor. It will get you out of a cooking bind every single time.

Parmesan cheese: Parmesan cheese has an excellent shelf life. While it does require refrigeration, a wedge of good-quality Parmesan can last for months. Store it loosely wrapped in parchment paper and then wrapped in plastic wrap. IAfter you've grated the cheese, save the rind and add it to soups, stocks, and stews for flavor and body.

Butter: A.k.a., the best ingredient ever! Butter is so luscious; it makes any recipe feel luxurious. I tend to gravitate to Kerrygold butter because it has a high fat content. Buy it in bulk, and keep it in the freezer.

OILS & VINEGARS

Extra-virgin olive oil: This is my everyday oil. I sauté, roast, and occasionally garnish with it. Olive oil stored in a dark glass bottle or aluminum has the best shelf life.

Canola oil or vegetable oil: These oils are best for high-heat cooking, like frying.

Vinegar: Vinegar brings balance and brightness. Lighter varieties like apple cider vinegar, red wine vinegar, and white wine vinegar can be used interchangeably.

Balsamic vinegar: Balsamic vinegar has a darker color and a sweeter, more robust flavor than other vinegars.

PRODUCE

These produce items make the cut as "staples" because of their long shelf life. When stored in a cool, dry place, they will last for weeks and weeks of meals.

Onions: The recipes in this book specify color, but yellow, white, and red onions can be used interchangeably in a pinch.

Potatoes: Both sweet potatoes and russet potatoes are suited for long-term storage, and they can even be used interchangeably in some recipes.

CONDIMENTS & SAUCES

Soy sauce: Soy sauce is not just for Asian cooking. I have immense appreciation for the Asian culinary masterminds that developed this kind of umami. Soy sauce is an excellent replacement for salt in a lot of applications.

Worcestershire sauce: Game changer. Worcestershire sauce has a little bit of everything in it. That's why it works so well in so many things.

Honey: Honey doesn't have an expiration date. It's true! When honey begins to crystallize, place the bottle in a mug of hot water to gently warm it up.

Mustard: The recipes in this book call for either Dijon or yellow mustard. I recommend using the type of mustard specified in each recipe, but if you have to pick just one mustard, go with Dijon.

RICE, BEANS, & PASTA

Rice: Long-grain rice (white or brown) is the priority; I always have a bag or two on hand. You can swap brown rice for white rice in recipes, but keep in mind that brown rice has a longer cook time.

Dried beans: Always keep a bag or two of dried beans on hand. My favorites are black-eyed peas, pinto beans, and kidney beans. They last forever, and they can be used in many dishes. Most bean recipes are flexible enough to swap one variety of beans for another; just try to stick with something similar to what is called for in the recipe.

Dried pasta: I keep a variety of pasta shapes on hand. You will find spaghetti, rigatoni, rotini, and lasagna noodles in my pantry. You can often swap one pasta shape for another, but try to use something similar to the recommended shape.

SEASONINGS & SPICES

Good food requires seasonings. The Staples List covers the essentials; for a full list of recommended seasonings, see page 16.

Kosher salt: Kosher salt is my all-purpose salt. The recipes in this book were developed using Diamond Crystal kosher salt, which is flakier and less salty than Morton kosher salt. If you find that recipes are too salty, consider switching to Diamond Crystal salt, or cut the salt measurement in half. I do not advise using iodized table salt.

Black pepper: Every recipe in this book was made with freshly ground black pepper. Invest in a pepper grinder or a coffee grinder so you can grind a small batch of whole peppercorns each week.

Granulated garlic: The flavor profile of granulated garlic is different from fresh garlic. It is a little sweeter and has a nutty quality. Granulated garlic and garlic powder are both made from dehydrated garlic, but I perfer granulated garlic because its coarse texture makes it less likely to clump.

Onion powder: Onion powder is a bit sweeter than fresh onion and doesn't have the same "sting." Onion powder can serve as the primary layer of onion or be added as an additional layer of flavor to fresh onion.

Paprika: Smoked paprika is always at the top of my list. If a recipe calls specifically for smoked paprika, try to use it. Sweet paprika is sufficient for all other applications.

Nice-to-Have Spices and Seasonings

This is a complete list of the dried herbs, spices, and seasonings I like to keep on hand. You just might find that they become staples in your pantry or spice cabinet, too.

SPICES
- ○ Ground allspice
- ○ Ground cardamom
- ○ Cayenne
- ○ Chili powder
- ○ Ground cinnamon
- ○ Ground cumin
- ○ Granulated garlic
- ○ Kosher salt
- ○ Mushroom powder
- ○ Onion powder
- ○ Paprika (smoked and sweet)
- ○ Red pepper flakes
- ○ Ground turmeric

WHOLE SPICES
- ○ Bay leaves
- ○ Black peppercorns
- ○ Cardamom pods
- ○ Cinnamon sticks
- ○ Coriander seeds
- ○ Nutmeg
- ○ Sesame seeds
- ○ Vanilla bean pods

DRIED HERBS
- ○ Basil
- ○ Chives
- ○ Lavender
- ○ Oregano
- ○ Parsley
- ○ Rosemary
- ○ Thyme

BLENDS
- ○ Chinese five spice
- ○ Curry powder
- ○ Grill seasoning
- ○ Herbes de Provence
- ○ Italian seasoning
- ○ YoungBae seasoning (FoodLoveTog) or Old Bay

FOR FUN
- ○ Black sesame seeds
- ○ Granulated honey
- ○ Maldon flaky sea salt
- ○ Pink peppercorns
- ○ Smoked sea salt
- ○ Vinegar powder

Equipment List

Good quality kitchen equipment can alleviate a lot of frustration in the kitchen. Most items on this list will last a very long time if cared for properly. Invest in quality products made by trusted brands when you are able. I consider these items everyday pieces of equipment in my kitchen.

FOR PREP

- Colander
- Cutting board
- Dry measuring cups
- Food processor
- Knife (I prefer a Santoku knife over a chef's knife, but go with what's most comfortable. Keep it clean, and keep it sharp.)
- Liquid measuring cups
- Mandoline
- Mixing bowls
- Pastry brush
- Rolling pin
- Rubber spatula
- Stand mixer or hand mixer
- Wooden spoon
- Zester/grater

FOR COOKING

- Aluminum foil
- Baking sheets
- Baking rack
- Candy thermometer
- 10-inch (25cm) cast-iron skillet
- 12-inch (30.5cm) cast-iron skillet
- Dutch oven or other heavy-bottomed pot
- Fish spatula
- Glass or cast-iron pie dish
- Loaf pan
- Parchment paper
- Slotted spoon or kitchen spider
- Tongs
- 9 × 13-inch (23 × 33cm) baking dish

FOR STORAGE

- Airtight food-storage containers
- Food-storage bags
- Freezer-safe food-storage bags
- Plastic wrap

Appetizers & Snacks

Black-Eyed Pea Salsa

I've always had an affinity for black-eyed peas. As a child, they were the only "bean" I would eat. As an adult, I have learned how versatile black-eyed peas are, and I enjoy eating them in many different ways. This salsa is excellent with tortilla chips, but it's also incredibly delicious as a topping for grilled chicken or roasted salmon.

Prep time **20 minutes** • Cook time **none** • Yield **4 cups** • Serving size **¼ cup**

¼ cup balsamic vinegar

2 tbsp extra-virgin olive oil

2 tsp kosher salt

1 tsp granulated garlic

½ tsp paprika

½ tsp freshly ground black pepper

1 tbsp granulated sugar (optional)

1 (15oz; 425g) can plain black-eyed peas, drained and rinsed

⊕ ½ cup diced red bell pepper

⊕ ½ cup diced green bell pepper

⊕ ½ cup diced orange bell pepper

1 small red onion, finely diced

⊕ 1 cup quartered grape or cherry tomatoes

⊕ ½ cup minced flat-leaf parsley

1. In a large bowl, whisk together the vinegar, oil, salt, garlic, paprika, pepper, and sugar, if using.

2. Add the black-eyed peas, bell peppers, onion, tomatoes, and parsley, and toss gently until combined. Serve immediately, or chill until ready to serve.

VARIATION

This recipe also works with other varieties of beans. If using black beans, replace the balsamic vinegar with an equivalent quantity of lime juice.

Sweet Potato Hummus

Sweet potato is a fun variation on hummus that includes warm spices, perfect for fall. The bright orange from the sweet potato blends perfectly with flecks of cinnamon and cardamom throughout this thick and creamy dip. A bit of sweetness and a bit of tanginess create a perfectly balanced bite. I serve this with pretzel rods and fresh veggies.

Prep time **30 minutes** • Cook time **15 minutes** • Yield **3 cups** • Serving size **2 tbsp**

1 large sweet potato, peeled

3 cloves garlic, minced

3 tbsp extra-virgin olive oil, divided

2½ tsp kosher salt, divided

1 tsp freshly ground black pepper, divided

¼ cup tahini

1 (15oz; 425g) can chickpeas, drained and rinsed

1 tsp smoked paprika

½ tsp ground cinnamon

½ tsp ground cardamom

¼ tsp cayenne (optional)

Juice of 1 lemon

¼ cup water

1. Preheat the oven to 400°F (200°C). While the oven is preheating, cut the sweet potatoes into bite-sized pieces. In a large bowl, toss the sweet potatoes with the garlic, 1 tablespoon olive oil, ½ teaspoon salt, and ½ teaspoon black pepper until evenly coated. Spread the sweet potatoes evenly on a baking sheet, and bake for 12 to 15 minutes or until fork-tender. Let cool for 5 to 10 minutes before proceeding.

2. In a food processor, combine the roasted sweet potatoes, tahini, chickpeas, paprika, cinnamon, cardamom, cayenne (if using), and the remaining 2 tablespoons olive oil, 2 teaspoons salt, and ½ teaspoon black pepper. Blend until smooth. Add the lemon juice, and then add the water 1 tablespoon at a time, blending between each addition until the hummus reaches your desired consistency.

NOTE
To store, drizzle 1 tablespoon olive oil on top, and refrigerate in an airtight container for up to 2 weeks.

VARIATIONS
No sweet potatoes? You can follow the same method using 3 large carrots or 1 small butternut squash, peeled and chopped.

White beans can be used in place of chickpeas, if needed.

Jack's Guacamole

When my sweet friend Erin was pregnant, she requested my guacamole so often that I joked with her that baby Jack was going to come out green. That is how my guacamole recipe became Jack's Guacamole. An obscene amount of lime juice and red onion is what sets this guac apart from all others.

Prep time **20 minutes** • Cook time **none** • Yield **2½ cups** • Serving size **3 tbsp**

- 3 avocados
- Juice of 1½ limes
- 1 small red onion, diced
- 1 jalapeño, seeded and finely diced
- ½ cup chopped fresh cilantro
- 1 tbsp kosher salt
- 1 tsp freshly ground black pepper

1. Begin by cutting each avocado in half. Twist the avocado to separate each half, then remove the pit by carefully pressing your knife into the pit and twisting it out. Discard the pit. Use the knife to slice lines into the flesh of the avocado horizontally, then vertically. Do not cut through the skin. Use a spoon to scoop out the grid of avocado flesh into a medium bowl. Squeeze the limes over the avocado.

2. Add the onion, jalapeño, cilantro, salt, and pepper, and toss the mixture until evenly distributed. Use a fork or potato masher to gently mash the avocado, breaking up some of the cubes to form a paste. Stir until well mixed; the guacamole should have a chunky texture with solid cubes of avocado.

NOTES

For a smoother texture, continue mashing the avocado with a fork or potato masher until you've reached the desired consistency.

To store, press plastic wrap directly onto the surface of the guacamole. Refrigerate for up to 3 days.

VARIATION

Add ½ cup diced mango for a little extra sweetness. Add a diced habañero for extra heat.

Parmesan Crisps

Despite their fancy name, these lacy baked cheese crisps could not be easier to make. Use them as an elegant garnish for soups or salads, or just eat them on their own. They might replace chips in your pantry if you're not careful!

Prep time **15 minutes** • Cook time **5 minutes** • Yield **10 crisps** • Serving size **2 crisps**

1 (4oz; 110g) wedge
Parmesan cheese

1. Preheat the oven to 375°F (190°C). Line a baking sheet with parchment paper. Using a Microplane grater or the smallest holes on a box grater, grate the cheese into a small bowl until you have about 1 cup grated cheese. (Do not use preshredded Parmesan; it will not melt properly.)

2. Scoop the grated cheese into 10 small mounds on the prepared baking sheet, about 1½ tablespoons of cheese per mound, leaving a little space between each. Lightly pat each mound to flatten slightly.

3. Place the baking sheet on the center rack of the oven, and bake for 5 to 7 minutes. Allow the crisps to cool for 2 to 3 minutes before gently removing them from the baking sheet with an offset spatula or fish spatula.

NOTE
Store crisps in an airtight container for up to 2 weeks. Do not refrigerate. (The crisps will become soggy.)

VARIATION
There is quite a bit of creative freedom in making these. You can play with seasonings and even try another type of cheese. Try using cheddar cheese, or consider stirring in 1 tablespoon red pepper flakes, dried rosemary, or everything bagel seasoning to enhance the flavor of your crisps.

Pico de Salsa

This simple salsa has the fresh flavor of pico de gallo with a blended, restaurant-style salsa texture. That's it! There aren't any magic ingredients, and there's nothing overly complicated. Just bright, fresh ingredients that blend perfectly to accompany a bowl of tortilla chips or to top your Turkey Taco Skillet (page 84).

Prep time **20 minutes** • Cook time **none** • Yield **1½ cups** • Serving size **2 tbsp**

- 5 vine-ripened tomatoes
- 1 small red onion
- 1 jalapeño, seeds removed
- ½ cup chopped fresh cilantro
- Juice of 2 limes
- 1 tsp honey
- 1 tbsp kosher salt
- 1 tsp freshly ground black pepper

1. Slice off the tops and stems of each tomato. Gently squeeze out the juice and seeds and discard. Set 1 tomato aside. Cut the remaining seeded tomatoes into pieces. Place the tomato pieces into a food processor, and pulse 5 to 7 times until only a few large chunks remain. The mixture should resemble canned petite-diced tomatoes. Transfer the processed tomatoes to a medium bowl. Cut the remaining tomato into ¼-inch (.5cm) pieces, and stir the pieces into the processed tomatoes.

2. Cut the red onion and jalapeño into large chunks. Return the food processor bowl to its base, and add the red onion, jalapeño, and cilantro. Pulse the food processor 5 to7 times until the ingredients are cut into fine pieces. Add the processed vegetables to the bowl with the tomatoes, and stir until combined.

3. Stir in the lime juice, honey, salt, and pepper until well blended.

NOTES
This salsa should be just slightly chunky. Take care not to over process the ingredients.

Salsa can be served cold or at room temperature.

To store, refrigerate in an airtight container for up to 2 weeks.

Loaded Potato Skins

As a kid, I always wanted my family to order potato skins as an appetizer at restaurants. They've fallen out of favor in recent years, but I'm on a mission to change that. I've taken this forgotten classic and revamped it with savory, tender caramelized onions and an amped-up sour cream sauce. If you ever have leftover baked potatoes, make these.

Prep time **10 minutes** • Cook time **1 hour 10 minutes** • Yield **12 potato skins** • Serving size **2 potato skins**

6 small russet potatoes

1½ tbsp vegetable or canola oil

6 strips bacon, chopped

1 tbsp butter

2 small yellow onions, thinly sliced

2 cloves garlic, minced

1 tsp Worcestershire sauce

1 tsp kosher salt

½ tsp freshly ground black pepper

⊕ 1½ cups shredded cheddar cheese

⊕ 3 tbsp chopped scallions or chives, to garnish

For the sauce

⊕ 1 cup sour cream

⊕ 2 tbsp **Savory Dry Rub** (page 135)

1 tsp Worcestershire sauce

1. Preheat the oven to 425°F (220°C). Line a baking sheet with foil. Rinse each potato, carefully scrubbing off any dirt or residue. Pat each potato dry with paper towels, and use a fork to poke a few holes in the skins. Place the potatoes on the prepared baking sheet, and rub each one with oil. Bake for 45 to 60 minutes. The potatoes are done when they are fork-tender and the potato skin is crispy. Set aside to cool for 15 to 20 minutes.

2. Meanwhile, in a medium skillet, cook the bacon over medium heat for 12 to 15 minutes until fully cooked and crisp. Transfer to a paper towel–lined plate to drain. Set aside.

3. Pour the rendered bacon fat into a heat-safe bowl, leaving about 1 tablespoon in the pan. Return the skillet to medium-low heat, and melt the butter. Add the onion and garlic. Cook for 20 to 30 minutes, stirring occasionally, until the onions are tender and golden brown. Stir in the Worcestershire, salt, and pepper. Remove from the heat and set aside.

4. To make the sauce, in a small bowl, combine all ingredients. Cover and refrigerate until ready to use.

5. Cut the cooled potatoes in half lengthwise, and scoop out the potato flesh, leaving about ¼ inch (.5cm) of flesh in the skin. (Discard the potato flesh, or reserve for another purpose; see note.)

6. Place each potato skin back on the baking sheet. Using a pastry brush, brush a little of the rendered bacon fat into the flesh of each potato skin. Into each potato skin, spoon about 2 tablespoons of caramelized onions and top with shredded cheddar. Bake for 5 to 7 minutes or until the cheese has melted. Top each potato skin with bacon and a dollop of the sauce. Garnish with chopped scallions.

NOTE
The leftover potato can be used for Garlic Parmesan Mashed Potatoes (page 107) or Easy Potato Soup (page 56).

Candied Bacon

Believe it or not, there is a way to upgrade bacon. I know it's hard to believe because bacon is the most fantastic thing ever, but there is a way to make it better. Candied bacon is the perfect combination of sweet and salty, and it requires only two ingredients. It's great for breakfast or as a snack. Serve it when you host a brunch, and I promise it will be the first thing to disappear. I personally love it on The Best BLT (page 52).

Prep time **10 minutes** • Cook time **15–20 minutes** • Yield **6–8 strips bacon** • Serving size **2 strips bacon**

8oz (225g) thick-cut bacon

3 tbsp brown sugar

1. Line a large baking sheet with aluminum foil or parchment paper. Place the bacon on the baking sheet in a single layer, leaving a bit of space between each strip.

2. Place the bacon in a cold oven (not preheated). Set the oven to 400°F (200°C). Set a timer for 10 minutes. After 10 minutes, remove the baking sheet from the oven.

3. Sprinkle the brown sugar over the bacon. Press the sugar into the bacon, spreading it so that it coats each strip evenly. Return the baking sheet to the oven, and cook for 8 to 10 minutes or until the bacon is fully cooked.

4. Let cool for 5 minutes before removing the bacon from the baking sheet, but don't allow it to cool completely. (Too much cooling time will cause the bacon to stick.) Place the slightly cooled bacon on a paper towel–lined plate until ready to serve.

NOTE
You may notice the brown sugar burning on the foil around the bacon. That's okay as long as the sugar on the bacon isn't burning.

VARIATION
For a little heat, sprinkle the bacon with freshly ground black pepper or red pepper flakes after adding the brown sugar.

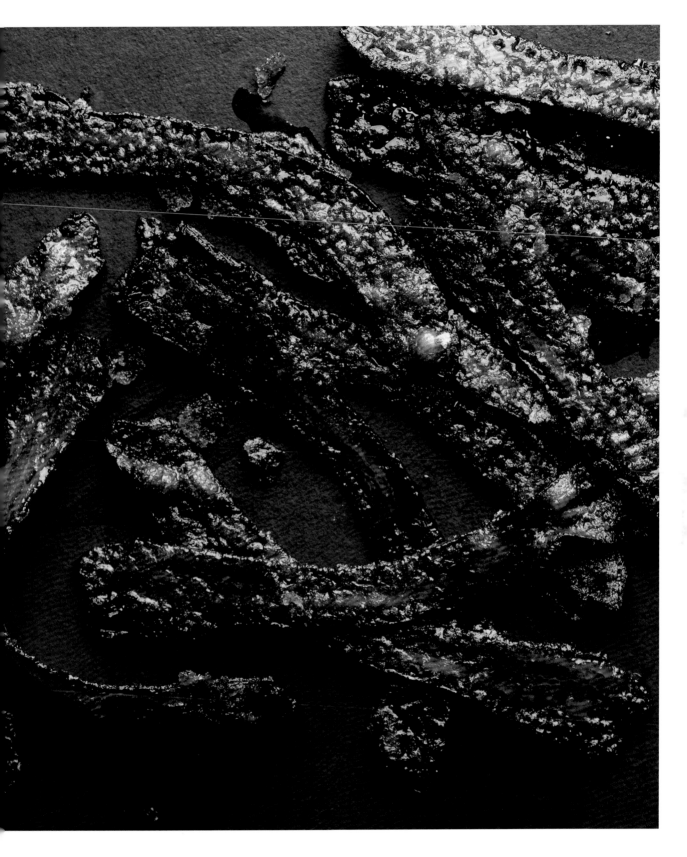

Bacon-Wrapped Dates

These dates disappear so quickly, you'd better make extra. Every single time I offer these as an appetizer, people are sad there aren't more. The assembly requires a little effort, but the result is well worth it. The combination of the sweet dates, salty bacon, and tangy cream cheese pleases every part of the palate. Just trust me; make extra.

Prep time **30 minutes** • Cook time **20–25 minutes** • Yield **24 dates** • Serving size **2–3 dates**

⊕ 6oz (170g) cream cheese, softened

½ tsp granulated garlic

½ tsp smoked paprika

⊕ 1 tsp minced fresh thyme, divided

1 tsp kosher salt, divided

½ tsp freshly ground black pepper, divided

⊕ 24 pitted Medjool dates

12 strips bacon, cut in half

¼ cup honey

⊕ ⅓ cup shelled pistachios

1. Preheat the oven to 400°F (200°C). Line a baking sheet with parchment paper.

2. In a small bowl, combine the cream cheese, granulated garlic, paprika, ½ teaspoon thyme, ½ teaspoon salt, and ¼ teaspoon pepper. Mix until the seasonings are fully blended into the cream cheese.

3. Split the dates in half lengthwise without cutting through the date. Stuff each date with the cream cheese mixture, and gently squeeze until sealed. Wrap each date with bacon, and place them seam side down on the prepared baking sheet. Repeat with the remaining dates until they are all stuffed and wrapped.

4. In a small bowl, combine the honey and the remaining ½ teaspoon thyme, ½ teaspoon salt, and ¼ teaspoon pepper. Drizzle half of the honey mixture over the dates. Place the dates in the oven for 20 to 25 minutes until the bacon is fully cooked and slightly crisp.

5. Meanwhile, in a dry skillet over medium-low heat, toast the pistachios for 3 to 5 minutes or until they are lightly browned. You will be able to smell them before you can see they are ready. Keep a watchful eye, as they can go from perfectly toasted to burnt very quickly. Cool for 2 to 3 minutes, and then chop finely.

6. Remove the dates from the oven, and drizzle with the remaining honey. Garnish with chopped pistachios. Serve warm.

NOTES

Don't worry if the honey in the pan around the dates begins to burn a bit; it will stay behind on the parchment paper.

Prep the dates ahead, and refrigerate until ready to bake. Drizzle the honey over the dates just before putting them in the oven.

To store, refrigerate in an airtight container for up to 1 week. Reheat in a 400°F (200°C) oven for 5 minutes.

Sweet & Spicy Pecans

I come from a Southern family, so I know a thing or two about pecans. Made with brown sugar and maple syrup, as well as a blend of warm and savory spices, these pecans are the perfect balance of sweet, spicy, and savory. They're excellent as a simple snack and will enhance any charcuterie board.

Prep time **15 minutes** • Cook time **12 minutes** • Yield **2 cups** • Serving size **¼ cup**

- 2 cups pecan halves
- 4 tbsp butter
- 3 tbsp brown sugar
- 1 tbsp maple syrup
- 2 tsp ground cinnamon
- 1 tbsp kosher salt
- 1 tsp granulated garlic
- 1 tsp paprika
- 1 tsp ground ginger
- ½ tsp chili powder
- ¼ tsp cayenne (optional)

1. Preheat the oven to 400°F (200°C). Line a baking sheet with foil.

2. Spread the pecan halves on the prepared baking sheet in a single layer. Place the baking sheet in the oven for 2 to 3 minutes to lightly toast the pecans. Remove the baking sheet from the oven, and transfer the pecans to a medium bowl.

3. In a small microwave-safe bowl, melt the butter. Stir in the sugar, syrup, cinnamon, salt, granulated garlic, paprika, ginger, chili powder, and cayenne, if using. Pour the butter mixture over the pecans, and toss until fully coated.

4. Return the pecans to the foil-lined baking sheet and arrange them in a single layer. Roast the pecans for 7 to 10 minutes. The sugar coating should be caramelized and bubbling. Remove the pecans from the oven, and allow them to cool slightly before transferring them to a bowl or an airtight container.

NOTE
Store pecans in an airtight container in a cool, dry place for up to 2 weeks.

VARIATION
This method can be used with other nut varieties, such as almonds, walnuts, or cashews.

Crispy Oven-Baked Chicken Wings

Chicken wings are a household staple for me. I make them often, and I make a lot of them. Pulling out the fryer and oil became a bit daunting, so I came up with a way to make a baked version that tastes even better than fried wings. Thanks to a longer cooking process, these wings are flavorful and succulent, with tender meat and crispy skin. They're sure to be on regular rotation in your house, too.

Prep time **15 minutes** • Cook time **1 hour** • Yield **24 pieces** • Serving size **6 pieces**

- 12 whole chicken wings, broken down into flats and drumettes (see note)
- 2 tbsp canola oil
- 1½ tbsp kosher salt
- ½ tsp freshly ground black pepper
- 1 tsp granulated garlic
- 1 tsp smoked paprika
- ½ tsp onion powder
- **Parmesan Ranch** (optional, page 126), to serve

1. Line a baking sheet with paper towel. Arrange the chicken pieces on the prepared baking sheet in a single layer, and let them sit at room temperature for least 20 minutes or up to 1 hour. Do not refrigerate. (This brings the chicken to room temperature and allows the skin to dry out a bit. This step is critical to achieving crispy skin.)

2. Preheat the oven to 400°F (200°C). Line a baking sheet with foil, and then place an oven-safe baking rack on the foil-lined baking sheet.

3. Place the chicken in a large bowl. Drizzle the oil over the chicken and sprinkle with the salt, pepper, granulated garlic, paprika, and onion powder. Toss until each piece is evenly coated in oil and seasonings. Arrange the chicken on the baking rack, leaving space between each piece. Bake for 1 hour. (You do not need to flip the chicken while baking if you use a baking sheet fitted with a baking rack.) Serve hot with Parmesan Ranch for dipping, if desired.

NOTE
I prefer to purchase whole chicken wings and break them down into drumettes, flats (or wingettes), and tips by cutting at the joints. The wing tips can be frozen and used for Homemade Chicken Stock (page 124).

VARIATIONS
Get creative with your seasonings! Try using Savory Dry Rub (page 135) or Taco Seasoning (page 135) in place of the seasonings in this recipe. For saucy wings, toss the chicken in BBQ Sauce (page 132) after baking.

If you have bacon fat on hand, replace 1 tablespoon canola oil with 1 tablespoon bacon fat for added flavor.

Hush Puppies

The perfect hush puppy is golden brown and crispy on the outside and fluffy like a pillow on the inside. These little babies are essentially fried cornbread, but require a bit of technique to master. Be sure to use cold butter to ensure that they puff up and stay crisp on the outside. A well-seasoned batter makes these the perfect accompaniment to fried fish, BBQ, and more.

Prep time **20 minutes** • Cook time **20 minutes** • Yield **15–20 hush puppies** • Serving size **2 hush puppies**

6 cups vegetable or canola oil, for frying

1 cup all-purpose flour

1 cup finely ground cornmeal

2 tbsp granulated sugar

1½ tsp baking powder

2 tsp kosher salt

1 tsp granulated garlic

1 tsp onion powder

¼ tsp freshly ground black pepper

4 tbsp cold butter, cut into pieces

⊕ 1 cup whole-milk buttermilk

⊕ 1 egg

¼ cup finely diced yellow onion

1. In a large Dutch oven or other heavy-bottomed pot, heat the oil over medium-high heat. Use a candy thermometer to regulate the temperature to 350°F (175°C).

2. In a large bowl, whisk together the flour, cornmeal, sugar, baking powder, salt, granulated garlic, onion powder, and pepper. Using a pastry cutter (or two forks), cut the cold butter into the cornmeal mixture until the mixture crumbles and resembles sand with pea-sized pieces of butter.

3. In a large liquid measuring cup, measure the buttermilk. Add the egg to the buttermilk, and whisk until the egg is thoroughly beaten and no streaks of yolk remain. Gently stir the buttermilk mixture into the dry ingredients until a smooth batter forms. Fold in the onion, taking care not to overmix the batter.

4. Use a medium cookie scoop (about 2 tablespoons) to carefully drop balls of batter into the hot oil. Work in batches, dropping no more than 5 to 7 balls at a time. Cook for 5 minutes, turning the hush puppies frequently using a slotted spoon or kitchen spider to ensure browning on all sides. The hush puppies are done when they have puffed slightly and turned golden brown. Remove the hush puppies from the hot oil, and drain on a baking sheet fitted with a baking rack or paper towel–lined plate.

NOTES
Serve warm with Homemade Tartar Sauce (page 127).

Store in an airtight container in the refrigerator. To reheat, warm in a 400°F (200°C) oven for 3 to 5 minutes.

VARIATION
Jazz up your hush puppy batter by adding 2 tablespoons chopped chives, ½ cup shredded cheddar cheese, or a diced jalapeño.

Classic Deviled Eggs

My family tends to have deviled eggs at every holiday celebration, especially during the spring and summer months. There has always been a great debate over whether the filling should be on the sweet side or the savory side. My vote is for the savory side, with capers and fresh dill. You can save that sweet pickle relish for your hot dog.

Prep time **40 minutes** • Cook time **13 minutes** • Yield **24 deviled eggs** • Serving size **2 deviled eggs**

- 12 eggs
- ½ cup mayonnaise (for **Homemade Mayo,** see page 126)
- 2 tbsp Dijon mustard
- 1 tsp white wine vinegar
- 1 tsp honey
- 1 tbsp chopped capers + 2 tsp caper juice
- 2 tsp chopped fresh dill
- ½ tsp kosher salt
- ¼ tsp freshly ground black pepper
- Smoked paprika (optional), to garnish

1. To a large pot, add the eggs and enough cold water to cover the eggs by at least 2 inches (5cm). Bring to a boil over high heat, and immediately remove from the heat. Cover with a lid, and let sit for exactly 13 minutes. (No more, no less!)

2. Meanwhile, prepare an ice bath by filling a large bowl with ice and cold water. After 13 minutes, transfer the eggs to the ice bath to cool. (See note.)

3. When cool, carefully peel the eggs and slice them in half lengthwise. Set the whites aside, and place the yolks in a large bowl. To the bowl with the egg yolks, add the mustard, vinegar, honey, capers and caper juice, dill, salt, and pepper. Mix with a hand mixer or whisk vigorously until the filling is smooth.

4. Spoon the filling into a piping bag or gallon-sized food-storage bag and snip off the tip (corner) of the bag. Pipe the filling into each egg white. Sprinkle with smoked paprika to garnish, if desired.

NOTE
The ice bath is important; it stops the cooking process and keeps the eggs from developing an overcooked greenish-gray layer around the yolk, and it makes them easier to peel. To peel the eggs without damaging the whites, gently crack around all sides, and start to peel with the pad of your finger, not your nail.

VARIATIONS
The options for garnish are endless. Consider breaking up a few Parmesan Crisps (page 25) or strips of Candied Bacon (page 28) and placing a piece on top of each egg. If you want to get really fancy, top the eggs with a small piece of smoked salmon or a bit of caviar.

Butternut Squash Fritters

These squash fritters are a show-stopping dish, and no one has to know that the most challenging part of making them is peeling the squash. The rest is so easy and so minimal. These fritters are perfect as an appetizer or side dish. Serve them with Roasted Chicken with Root Veggies (page 69) or Pan-Seared Pork Chops with Pan Gravy (page 81).

Prep time **30 minutes** • Cook time **30 minutes** • Yield **12–15 fritters** • Serving size **2 fritters**

⊕ 1 large butternut squash
⅔ cup all-purpose flour
2 cloves garlic, minced
⊕ 2 eggs, beaten
⊕ 1 tbsp minced fresh sage
2 tsp kosher salt
1½ tsp granulated garlic
1 tsp onion powder
½ tsp freshly ground black pepper
3 tbsp extra-virgin olive oil

1. Using a vegetable peeler, peel the skin from the butternut squash. Cut the bottom curved part of the butternut squash off and scoop out the seeds. Cut both the bottom and top of the butternut squash into manageable pieces for a food processor. Using the shredding blade, shred the butternut squash in the food processor. (This can also be done on a box grater.)

2. In a large bowl, toss the shredded squash with the flour, minced garlic, eggs, sage, salt, granulated garlic, onion powder, and pepper until well combined.

3. Heat a large skillet over medium-high heat. When hot, add 1 tablespoon oil and swirl to coat. Scoop the squash mixture into the hot skillet, using approximately ¼ cup of the mixture for each fritter. Gently press down with the spoon to flatten each fritter. Work in batches, and cook no more than 4 to 5 fritters at a time. Cook for 3 to 4 minutes until golden brown on the bottom, and then flip and cook the opposite side for 2 to 3 minutes. Continue until all the fritters have been cooked, using 1 tablespoon oil for each batch.

4. Remove from the heat and sprinkle lightly with salt. Serve while the fritters are still hot.

NOTE
Top these beauties with a dollop of Bacon Jam (page 134).

VARIATION
You can make these fritters using 4 cups shredded potatoes or shredded sweet potatoes instead of butternut squash.

Apricot Gorgonzola Cheese Dip

This recipe name is a mouthful, right? It might even sound weird, but I need you to trust me. Every single time I make this, it's the first thing gone. Everyone loves it; everyone asks for the recipe; and some even lick the bowl. The combination of salty, pungent Gorgonzola cheese with sweet apricot and smoky bacon just works. It's perfect on a charcuterie board or served with crackers.

Prep time **10 minutes** • Cook time **10 minutes** • Yield **1½ cups** • Serving size **2 tbsp**

4 strips bacon

⊕ 8oz (28g) cream cheese, softened

⊕ ⅓ cup apricot preserves

⊕ ¼ cup crumbled Gorgonzola cheese

⊕ 3 scallions, chopped

½ tsp kosher salt

¼ tsp freshly ground black pepper

1. Heat a medium skillet over medium heat. Add the bacon, and cook for 10 to 12 minutes until fully cooked and crispy. Transfer to a paper towel–lined plate to cool. When cool, crumble the bacon into small bits.

2. In a medium bowl, combine the crumbled bacon with the cream cheese, preserves, Gorgonzola cheese, scallions, salt, and pepper, stirring until fully incorporated. Dip can be served at room temperature or chilled.

NOTES

Can't find Gorgonzola? You can make this with blue cheese.

To store, refrigerate in an airtight container for up to 1 week.

Mango Salsa

This versatile salsa hits all the flavor notes—sweet and tart, with just enough spice from the jalapeño. It's a favorite with my meal-prep clients because it adds a little sweetness without any sugar. Serve it with tortilla chips or with fish or grilled chicken. However you decide to eat it, it will always be light, refreshing, and tasty.

Prep time **20 minutes** • Cook time **none** • Yield **2 cups** • Serving size **2 tbsp**

- 2 ripe mangoes
- 1 jalapeño, seeded and diced
- ½ cup diced red onion
- ¼ cup chopped fresh cilantro
- Juice of 2 limes
- 1 tsp kosher salt

1. Slice off the sides of the mango, cutting vertically from top to bottom. Use a paring knife to cut a grid pattern on each mango half. Be careful not to cut through the skin. Press the underside of the mango to invert the flesh and grid pattern. Use a spoon to scoop out the mango flesh. You may find that you need to cut a few mango pieces smaller to ensure they are all similar in size.

2. In a large bowl, combine the diced mango with the jalapeño, onion, cilantro, lime juice, and salt. Toss until all ingredients are thoroughly coated with the lime juice. Serve immediately, or chill before serving.

NOTES
Serve with Cinnamon Sugar Chips (page 42) or BBQ Pork Belly Tacos (page 54).

To store, refrigerate in an airtight container for up to 5 days.

VARIATION
This recipe is excellent with 2½ cups diced pineapple or strawberries in place of the mango.

Chili-Lime Watermelon

Summertime during my childhood meant cold slices of watermelon with a sprinkle of salt on the watermelon flesh. That first bite on a hot summer day was bliss. The sweetness of the juicy watermelon paired with tangy salt was pure low-country culinary genius. This chili-lime version is an elevated twist on that simple summer treat.

Prep time **20 minutes** • Cook time **none** • Yield **12 wedges** • Serving size **1 wedge**

- 1 medium seedless watermelon
- 2 limes
- ¼ cup kosher salt
- 1 tbsp chili powder
- 1 tsp smoked paprika
- ¼ tsp cayenne (optional)

1. Cut the watermelon into wedges. (I like to leave the rind on, but if you prefer to cut off the rind, feel free.) Zest the limes into a shallow bowl. Squeeze the lime juice into a second shallow bowl.

2. To the bowl with the lime zest, add the salt, chili powder, paprika, and cayenne, if using. Stir until thoroughly mixed.

3. To assemble, dip each watermelon wedge into the lime juice, and then sprinkle about ¼ teaspoon of chili-lime salt onto each side. Serve chilled or at room temperature.

NOTES

This is not a make-ahead dish. Prepare this recipe right before you're ready to eat.

The chili-lime salt can be stored in an airtight container for up to 3 months. Use it to rim a margarita glass, or toss it onto freshly popped popcorn. It's also delicious on Mom's Corn on the Cob (page 95).

I prefer to leave the rind on my watermelon, but if you trim the rind, consider pickling it using the brine for Refrigerator Pickles (page 129).

Cinnamon Sugar Chips

This sweet snack is an ode to my childhood memories of eating my mom's cinnamon toast on Saturday mornings. Made with tortillas instead of bread, these chips are a bite-sized version of classic cinnamon sugar toast. You get to decide how sweet you want them—sprinkle as much or as little of the cinnamon sugar mixture as you'd like.

Prep time **10 minutes** • Cook time **10 minutes** • Yield **80 chips** • Serving size **8 chips**

3 tbsp ground cinnamon

¼ cup granulated sugar

10 (8in; 20cm) flour tortillas

4 tbsp butter, melted

1. Preheat the oven to 350°F (175°C). Line a baking sheet with parchment paper. In a small bowl, combine the cinnamon and sugar.

2. Cut each tortilla into 8 wedges and place the wedges in a large bowl. Drizzle the melted butter over the tortilla wedges, turning to coat, and sprinkle them with cinnamon sugar. Use as much or as little of the cinnamon sugar as you desire; you may end up with cinnamon sugar left over. Toss until the tortillas are fully covered in butter and cinnamon sugar.

3. Place the tortillas on the prepared baking sheet, and bake for 10 to 12 minutes or until golden brown.

NOTES

If you don't serve these with Apple Pie Dip (page 43), you are missing out! These are also great with Mango Salsa (page 39).

Keep an eye on these during the last 3 to 5 minutes of baking. The sugar can quickly go from sparkly to burnt.

Apple Pie Dip

When it comes to pie, I am a crust girl through and through, but this dip is a lovely surprise to serve at a gathering. You get all the sweet apple cinnamon flavor without the hassle of making a pie, and it requires little prep and cook time. Pair it with Cinnamon Sugar Chips (page 42) for apple pie vibes in every sense of the word.

Prep time **15 minutes** • Cook time **5–10 minutes** • Yield **1¼ cup** • Serving size **3 tbsp**

2 tbsp butter

⊕ 3 large apples, peeled and chopped into ¼-in (.5cm) pieces

½ cup granulated sugar

1 tsp ground cinnamon

⊕ ½ tsp ground nutmeg

½ tsp kosher salt

⊕ Juice of 1 lemon

⊕ ½ tsp pure vanilla extract (for **Vanilla Extract,** see page 137)

½ tbsp cornstarch

3 tbsp water

1. In a medium skillet, melt the butter over medium heat. Add the apples, and sauté for 2 to 3 minutes until the apples start to become tender. Stir in the sugar, cinnamon, nutmeg, and salt, and cook for 1 minute. Add the lemon juice and vanilla, and stir until combined.

2. In a small bowl, whisk the cornstarch and water with a fork until the cornstarch is fully dissolved. Pour the cornstarch slurry into the apple mixture, and increase the heat to medium-high. Stir until thoroughly combined. The apple mixture will begin to thicken. Reduce the heat to low, and continue cooking for 1 to 2 minutes.

3. Remove the apple mixture from the heat, and pour into a heat-safe bowl to serve. The dip will continue to thicken as it cools.

NOTES

For more flavor, sprinkle in ½ teaspoon of ground cardamom or ground allspice with the other spices in step 1.

Serve with Cinnamon Sugar Chips (page 42), graham crackers, or wafer cookies.

To store, refrigerate in an airtight container for up to 2 weeks.

Main Dishes

The Perfect Pancake

Pancakes are the first thing I think of the morning of my birthday. They are the food I crave when I'm not feeling well. Pancakes also remind me of my Grandma Lillie; she made them for us all the time. I love this recipe because it's absolutely perfect plain, but it can easily be enhanced with fresh berries, chocolate chips, crumbled bacon, and more.

Prep time **20 minutes** • Cook time **20 minutes** • Yield **6–8 pancakes** • Serving size **2–3 pancakes**

1½ cups all-purpose flour

2 tsp baking powder

½ tsp kosher salt

3 tbsp granulated sugar

⊕ 1 large egg, beaten

⊕ 1 cup whole-milk buttermilk

⊕ 3 tbsp butter, melted, plus more for the pan

1. In a medium bowl, whisk together the flour, baking powder, salt, and sugar. In a large liquid measuring cup, whisk together the egg, buttermilk, and melted butter. Stir the buttermilk mixture into the flour mixture, being sure not to overmix. (There should still be lumps but no signs of dry ingredients throughout the batter.) Let the batter rest for 10 to 15 minutes.

2. Heat a griddle or nonstick skillet over medium-low heat. Add 1 tablespoon butter to the skillet and allow to melt. Working in batches, add ¼-cup scoops of batter to the skillet. (For larger pancakes, add ½-cup scoops.) Cook until bubbles form on the wet surface of the pancake. When the bubbles begin to burst, flip and cook the opposite side until golden brown. Transfer to a plate or tray tented with foil. Continue cooking in batches, using 1 tablespoon of butter per batch, until all the batter is used.

NOTES

Don't skip the rest time. Letting the batter rest allows the flour to hydrate and the leavening agent to evenly distribute throughout the batter. This is what gives you light and fluffy pancakes!

For supercrispy pancake edges, cook them using 1 tablespoon coconut oil and 1 tablespoon butter.

VARIATION

To amp up your pancakes, sprinkle berries, chocolate chips, or crumbled bacon on the wet side of the pancake while the first side is cooking.

Bacon & Sweet Potato Hash
WITH OVER-EASY EGGS

Breakfast is one of my favorite things to make. I especially love breakfast for dinner, and this recipe is perfect for that. Apple and sweet potatoes give this hash a slight sweetness that's perfectly balanced by the savory flavors of bacon, onion, and garlic. Serve it alongside a Flaky, Fluffy Cream Cheese Biscuit (page 88) covered with jam.

Prep time **20 minutes** • Cook time **30 minutes** • Yield **6 cups hash + 4 eggs** • Serving size **1½ cups hash + 1 egg**

2 tbsp extra-virgin olive oil or coconut oil

6 strips thick-cut bacon, chopped

1 small yellow onion, chopped

2 cloves garlic, minced

2 sweet potatoes, peeled and cut into bite-sized pieces

1 tsp ground cinnamon

⊕ 1 tsp freshly ground nutmeg

3 tsp kosher salt, divided

¾ tsp freshly ground black pepper, divided

⊕ 1 apple, chopped

4 tbsp butter, divided

⊕ 4 eggs

⊕ Sliced avocado (optional), to garnish

1. Heat a large skillet over medium heat. Add the olive oil and then add the bacon. Cook for 10 to 12 minutes or until fully cooked. Transfer the bacon to a paper towel–lined plate to drain, leaving behind the rendered fat. Add the onion and garlic to the pan, and sauté for 3 to 5 minutes or until the onion starts to become translucent.

2. Add the sweet potatoes to the pan, and stir until fully coated in the remaining oil. Cover with a lid, and cook for 7 minutes. Remove the lid, and stir to ensure the potatoes are not sticking. Color should be developing at this point, but the potatoes will not be fully cooked. Add the cinnamon, nutmeg, 2½ teaspoons salt, ½ teaspoon pepper, and apple. Toss until the potatoes and apples are fully coated in seasoning. Replace the lid, and cook for 5 minutes more.

3. Meanwhile, in a small skillet, melt 2 tablespoons butter over medium-low heat. Crack an egg into a small bowl, and then carefully pour it into the skillet, taking care not to break the yolk. Repeat with a second egg. Cover the skillet, and cook the eggs for 3 to 5 minutes until the whites are fully cooked and the yolk is beginning to firm but is still runny. Season the eggs with ¼ teaspoon salt and ⅛ teaspoon pepper. Repeat to cook the remaining 2 eggs with the remaining 2 tablespoons butter, ¼ teaspoon salt, and ⅛ teaspoon pepper.

4. Remove the hash from the heat. (The sweet potatoes should be fully cooked and tender.) Stir in the bacon. To serve, top the hash with an over-easy egg. Garnish with sliced avocado, if desired.

NOTE
Hash can be refrigerated in an airtight container for up to 1 week. Cook the eggs as needed when ready to serve.

VARIATION
For a sausage hash, replace the bacon with 8oz (226g) pork, chicken, or turkey sausage, and add 1 tablespoon oil when cooking the meat to ensure it does not stick. Using turkey bacon is not recommended.

Orange Cinnamon French Toast

The best French toast is fluffy on the inside, buttery and golden on the outside, and slightly crisp. French toast should never be soggy. This method works well with any thickly sliced bread, but I prefer sourdough or brioche. Both types of bread soak up the custard perfectly and take on great flavor from the warm spices and orange zest.

Prep time **15 minutes** • Cook time **30 minutes** • Yield **8 slices** • Serving size **2 slices**

8 tbsp butter, divided

2 eggs + 1 egg yolk

1 cup half and half

Zest and juice of 1 orange

½ cup granulated sugar

2 tsp ground cinnamon

½ tsp kosher salt

1 tsp pure vanilla extract (for **Vanilla Extract,** see page 137)

8 slices sourdough bread

1. Preheat the oven to 375°F (190°C). Melt 4 tablespoons butter, and let it cool slightly.

2. In a shallow bowl, whisk together the eggs, egg yolk, and half and half until thoroughly combined. The mixture should be foamy and resemble pale orange juice. Add the melted butter, orange zest and juice, and sugar. Continue whisking until the sugar begins to dissolve. Add the cinnamon, salt, and vanilla. Whisk until the cinnamon is evenly distributed.

3. In a large skillet, melt 1 tablespoon butter over medium heat. While the butter is melting, place 2 slices of bread into the custard mixture and soak for 20 to 30 seconds on each side. Lift the bread from the bowl, letting any excess liquid drip off. Gently place the soaked bread into the skillet. Cook for 2 to 3 minutes on each side. Transfer the French toast to a baking sheet. Repeat with the remaining bread and butter, whisking the custard between each batch to ensure the cinnamon and orange zest stay evenly distributed.

4. Place the baking sheet in the oven for 10 minutes. Serve hot.

NOTES

French toast slices can be popped in the toaster to reheat.

French toast is the perfect accompaniment to Bacon & Sweet Potato Hash (page 48) or Candied Bacon (page 28).

Refrigerate leftover French toast in an airtight container for up to 1 week.

VARIATION

This recipe works well with brioche bread, challah, or plain Texas toast. If using a softer bread like brioche or challah, soak the slices for just 5 to 10 seconds on each side.

Mushroom Lover's Quiche

Quiches are highly underrated, don't you think? I am content with quiche for breakfast, lunch, and dinner. Making a mushroom quiche was kind of a no-brainer for me. I've come across plenty of quiches filled with too many things, but a quiche with mushrooms doesn't require much else. Throw in a side of Candied Bacon (page 28), and I'm a happy girl!

Prep time **30 minutes** • Cook time **1 hour 30 minutes** • Yield **1 9-in (23cm) quiche** • Serving size **1 slice**

½ batch **Pantry Pie Crust** (page 147; omit the sugar)

1 tbsp extra-virgin olive oil

8oz (225g) portabella mushrooms, sliced

8oz (225g) white button mushrooms sliced

1 small yellow onion, finely diced

2 cloves garlic, minced

1 tsp Worcestershire sauce

2 tsp kosher salt

½ tsp freshly ground black pepper

6 large eggs

1 cup half and half

1½ cups grated Gruyère cheese

1. On a lightly floured surface, roll out the crust to about 10 inches (25cm). Carefully place the pie crust into a 9-inch (23cm) pie pan. Trim any excess pie crust from around the pie pan and form the crust's edge. Crimp the pie crust with a fork or your fingers. Using a fork, poke small holes throughout the bottom of the crust. Line the crust with parchment paper, and pour in ceramic pie weights (or small ball bearings or dried beans). Bake the pie crust for 25 minutes, and then remove it from the oven. Set aside to cool.

2. While the pie crust is cooling, heat a large skillet over medium heat. Coat the skillet with olive oil, and add the mushrooms. Cook for 20 minutes, stirring occasionally, until the mushrooms begin to brown on both sides. Add the onion and garlic, and continue to cook for 3 to 4 minutes until the onion becomes translucent. Stir in the Worcestershire, salt, and pepper. Set aside to cool.

3. In a medium bowl, whisk together the eggs and half and half. Stir in the cheese.

4. Spoon the cooled mushroom mixture into the baked pie crust. Slowly pour in the egg mixture. Bake for 45 to 50 minutes or until a knife inserted into the center of the quiche comes out clean. Let cool for at least 20 minutes before cutting. Serve warm or at room temperature.

NOTES

If you have fresh thyme, toss in a few sprigs while cooking the mushrooms. Be sure to remove the thyme stems before spooning the mixture into the crust.

Leftover quiche can be refrigerated in an airtight container for up to 3 days.

The Best BLT

I spend a lot of time making delicious food for others, but I don't often get to make extraordinary things for myself. One thing I do love to do is make myself a BLT. Even if I get home late, placing some bacon on a baking sheet and slicing a few tomatoes doesn't feel impossible. If I get a second wind, I even make a deliciously seasoned aioli. It makes my sandwich feel gourmet, and it makes me feel like I've taken care of myself.

Prep time   **15 minutes**   •   Cook time   **20 minutes**   •   Yield   **4 sandwiches**   •   Serving size   **1 sandwich**

1lb (450g) thick-cut bacon

⊕ 1 large greenhouse or heirloom tomato

⊕ 8 slices country white bread

⊕ 4 tbsp **Roasted Garlic Aioli** (page 127)

⊕ 1 cup baby arugula

1. Line a baking sheet with foil. Arrange the bacon on the prepared sheet, leaving a bit of space between the strips. Place the baking sheet in a cold oven, and set the oven to 400°F (200°C). After 15 to 20 minutes, the bacon should be crisp, golden, and delicious. (Make sure you pour the puddle of bacon fat left on the baking sheet into a container for later use.)

2. While the bacon is in the oven, slice the tomato into at least 8 slices, and toast the bread.

3. To assemble, spread ½ tablespoon aioli on each piece of toasted bread. Place one piece of bread on a cutting board, aioli side up, and top with about ¼ cup arugula. Place 2 tomato slices on top. (You may have to overlap them a bit.) Next, add 4 strips of bacon. (You may have to cut them in half and layer them to get them to fit properly on the bread.) Finally, top the sandwich with another slice of bread, aioli side down.

NOTES

I am a classic white sandwich bread person, but you can use any sliced bread you like. I encourage everyone to consider something other than iceberg for their sandwiches. Leaf lettuce or butter lettuce are great options if you aren't a fan of arugula.

You could get fancy and toast your bread on the stovetop using a skillet and butter or bacon fat. I find it a bit too decadent with the aioli, but if you don't like condiments, this is a great way to get additional flavor into your BLT.

VARIATIONS

A BLT is also excellent when made with Candied Bacon (page 28). You could also use Homemade Mayo (page 126). I've been known to sneak in some slices of avocado or an over-easy egg, too.

The Juiciest Turkey Burger You've Ever Had

Turkey burgers can be the worst! Am I right? If not cooked properly, they can be gritty and resemble a hockey puck. I hardly ever order one at a restaurant because I know it's going to be an epic fail. Thankfully, I have figured out the best way to make a turkey burger. Full of flavor and crazy juicy, this will be the best turkey burger you have ever eaten.

Prep time **20 minutes** • Cook time **25 minutes** • Yield **4 burgers** • Serving size **1 burger**

- 1½lb (680g) 85/15 ground turkey
- 1 small red onion, chopped
- ½ cup chopped flat-leaf parsley
- 1 tbsp granulated garlic
- 2 tsp smoked paprika
- 2 tsp kosher salt
- 1 tsp freshly ground black pepper
- 1 tbsp extra-virgin olive oil
- 4 hamburger buns
- ¼ cup **Roasted Garlic Aioli** (page 127)
- 2 cups baby arugula

1. Preheat the oven to 400°F (200°C).

2. In a large bowl, combine the ground turkey, onion, parsley, garlic, paprika, salt, and pepper. Using your hands, mix until combined, taking care not to overmix. Form the turkey mixture into 4 patties, each about 6 ounces (170g).

3. Heat a cast-iron skillet over medium-high heat. Drizzle in oil to coat the bottom of the pan. Place the turkey patties into the skillet, and sear for 3 minutes until browned. Flip the patties, and sear on the opposite side for 1 minute. Carefully transfer the skillet to the oven, and cook for 15 minutes. (This will keep the burgers moist.) Do not overcook; if the patties are left in the oven for more than 20 minutes, they will become hard and dry.

4. Remove the skillet from the oven, and allow the patties to rest for a minimum of 15 minutes.

5. To assemble, split 1 tablespoon aioli between the top and bottom of a burger bun. Place ½ cup arugula on the bottom bun and place the burger patty on top. Place the top bun on the burger patty.

NOTES
Do not overmix the meat mixture. The warmth from your hands will start to break down the fat in the meat, which can lead to a dry burger patty.

Top this beauty with Caramelized Onions (page 130) or Refrigerator Pickles (page 129).

VARIATION
The same method can be used to make a beef burger.

BBQ Pork Belly Tacos

The words "tacos" and "pork belly" in the same recipe name just make sense. This combination is outstanding. The fattiness of the pork belly is balanced beautifully by the acidity of the pickled onions and the sweetness of the BBQ sauce, creating a flavor explosion like no other.

Prep time **10 minutes + 1 hour to marinate** • Cook time **35 minutes** • Yield **8 tacos** • Serving size **2 tacos**

2 cloves garlic, minced

⊕ 2 tbsp **Savory Dry Rub** (page 135)

1 tsp kosher salt

⊕ Zest and juice of 1 lime

2 tbsp honey

⊕ 2lb (1kg) pork belly, cut into 1½-in (3.5cm) cubes

⊕ ½ cup **BBQ Sauce** (page 132)

⊕ 8 flour tortillas, warmed

½ cup **Pickled Red Onions** (page 129)

Optional Toppings

⊕ 1 cup shredded green cabbage

⊕ 1 jalapeño, thinly sliced

1. In a large bowl, combine the garlic, dry rub, salt, lime zest and juice, and honey. Add the pork belly, and turn to coat evenly in marinade. Cover with plastic wrap, and refrigerate for 1 hour.

2. Preheat the oven to 400°F (200°C). Line a baking sheet with parchment paper. Spread the pork belly on the prepared baking sheet, leaving space between each piece. Roast for 20 minutes. Remove the baking sheet from the oven and flip each piece of meat. Return to the oven for 10 to 15 minutes more.

3. Using tongs, transfer the pork belly to a large bowl. Add the BBQ sauce to the bowl, and toss to coat. Return the pork belly to the parchment-lined baking sheet, and roast for 5 minutes more.

4. To assemble, place 2 to 3 pieces of pork belly in a warmed tortilla, and top with pickled red onions. Add shredded cabbage and jalapeño slices, if desired.

NOTE
Cooked pork belly pieces can be refrigerated in an airtight container for up to 1 week. To reheat, place in a 400°F (200°C) oven for 5 to 7 minutes or until heated through.

VARIATION
The pork belly is incredibly succulent and juicy on its own and can be made without the BBQ sauce. If you prefer to skip the sauce, remove the pork belly from the oven after 30 to 35 minutes of cooking, and omit step 3.

Easy Potato Soup

I have a little secret for you. This soup doesn't have to be made with fresh potatoes. You can use a bag of frozen shredded hash browns or diced potatoes. Or you could use the leftover potato flesh from Loaded Potato Skins (page 27). Bacon enhances the flavor for any interpretation, and celery and carrots provide wonderful texture. Have fun! Be bold. Make this recipe your own.

Prep time **30 minutes** • Cook time **45 minutes** • Yield **10 cups** • Serving size **2 cups**

6 strips bacon, chopped

1 large yellow onion, diced

2 carrots, diced

3 stalks celery, diced

3 cloves garlic, minced

1½ tsp granulated garlic

1 tsp onion powder

2 tbsp kosher salt

1 tsp freshly ground black pepper

2 large russet potatoes, peeled and cut into ½-in (1.25cm) cubes

2 bay leaves

3 sprigs fresh thyme

8 cups chicken stock, divided (for **Homemade Chicken Stock,** see page 124)

½ cup all-purpose flour

1½ cups shredded cheddar cheese, plus more to serve

½ cup heavy cream

1. Heat a large Dutch oven or other heavy-bottomed pot over medium heat. Add the bacon, and cook for 12 to 15 minutes until crisp. Using a slotted spoon, transfer the bacon to a paper towel–lined plate, leaving behind the rendered bacon fat.

2. Add the onion, carrots, celery, and minced garlic to the pot. Sauté over medium-high heat for 2 to 3 minutes until the vegetables are tender. Stir in the granulated garlic, onion powder, salt, and pepper. Add the potatoes, and stir until the seasonings are evenly distributed. Add the bay leaves, thyme, and 7½ cups chicken stock, and stir. Cover and cook over medium heat for 15 minutes or until the potatoes are tender.

3. Meanwhile, in a small bowl, whisk together the flour and the remaining ½ cup chicken stock to create a slurry. Remove the lid from the pot. Using tongs, remove the bay leaf and thyme stems. Increase the heat to medium-high. Slowly stir in the slurry while the soup is bubbling gently. The soup will begin to thicken. Reduce the heat to low, and cook uncovered for 10 minutes.

4. Stir in the cheddar cheese and heavy cream. Continue stirring until the cheese is melted and there are no more white streaks of cream. Remove from the heat. Serve topped with additional shredded cheese and crispy bacon.

NOTES

Cool to room temperature before storing. Refrigerate in an airtight container for up to 1 week.

Stir 1 tablespoon Caramelized Onions (page 130) into your soup for a little oniony sweetness. Meaty Mushrooms (page 114) are a great garnish.

Smoky Sweet Potato Soup

This one-pot wonder is luscious and smoky. It's full of vegetables, but the pickiest of eaters will never know because they are puréed down into velvety soup. Hearty sweet potatoes make it filling enough to be served as a meal, and when it's topped with candied bacon or toasted pumpkin seeds, it will feel like the easiest fancy soup you've ever made.

Prep time **30 minutes** • Cook time **30 minutes** • Yield **8 cups** • Serving size **1 cup**

1 tbsp extra-virgin olive oil

1 large yellow onion, chopped

2 celery stalks, chopped

2 large carrots, peeled and chopped

3 large sweet potatoes, peeled and cut into cubes

1 tbsp smoked paprika

½ tbsp granulated garlic

1 tbsp kosher salt

1 tsp freshly ground black pepper

2 sprigs fresh thyme

2 bay leaves

4½ cups chicken stock (for **Homemade Chicken Stock,** see page 124)

½ cup heavy cream

Candied Bacon (optional; page 28)

Toasted pumpkin seeds, pistachios, or pomegranate seeds (optional)

1. In a large pot, heat the oil over medium heat. Add the onion, celery, and carrots, and stir, being sure to coat all veggies with oil. Cook for 3 to 4 minutes until the onion and celery become translucent.

2. Add the sweet potatoes, and toss until everything is coated. Season with paprika, garlic, salt, and pepper. Stir until the seasonings are evenly distributed. Cook for 2 to 3 minutes.

3. Add the thyme and bay leaves and stir. Add the chicken stock, and increase the heat to bring to a boil. When boiling, reduce the heat to medium-low, and simmer for 15 to 20 minutes or until the sweet potatoes are tender.

4. Remove from the heat, and remove the thyme stems and bay leaves. Using an immersion blender, purée until smooth. (If you don't have an immersion blender, carefully blend the soup in batches in a regular blender.) Once blended, stir in the heavy cream. Serve topped with candied bacon pieces and toasted nuts or seeds, if using.

NOTES
Use bacon fat instead of olive oil if you have it.

Cool to room temperature before storing. Refrigerate in an airtight container for up to 1 week.

VARIATION
For a vegan version, replace the chicken stock with veggie stock and the heavy cream with full-fat coconut milk.

French Onion Soup

French onion soup comes to mind whenever I'm left with onions that need to be used before going bad. Caramelized onions and garlic create the base for a rich broth, full of umami, that's topped with toasty bread cubes and a mound of cheese. A humble ingredient transformed into something luxurious.

Prep time **20 minutes** • Cook time **1 hour** • Yield **8 cups** • Serving size **1½ cups**

½ cup butter

5 yellow onions, sliced

4 cloves garlic, minced

2 bay leaves

⊕ 1 baguette, cut into cubes

1 tbsp extra-virgin olive oil

2½ tsp kosher salt, divided

½ tsp freshly ground black pepper

⊕ 1 tbsp mushroom powder

1 tbsp Worcestershire sauce

2 tsp soy sauce

⊕ 2½ tsp anchovy paste

2 tbsp all-purpose flour

⊕ 6 cups beef stock

⊕ 1½ cups grated Gruyère cheese

1. Preheat the oven to 350°F (175°C).

2. In a large pot, melt the butter over medium heat. Add the onion and garlic. Cook for 10 minutes, stirring occasionally, until the onions begin to release their liquid. Add the bay leaves. Cook for 15 to 20 minutes, stirring occasionally, until the onions start to caramelize.

3. While the onions cook, spread the bread cubes on a baking sheet. Drizzle them with olive oil and season with ½ teaspoon salt. Place the baking sheet in the oven and toast the bread cubes for 10 to 15 minutes. The cubes should be browned and firm. Remove from the oven, and set aside to cool.

4. Remove the bay leaves from the pot, and add the remaining 2 teaspoons salt, pepper, mushroom powder, Worcestershire sauce, soy sauce, and anchovy paste, stirring until the paste begins to dissolve. Add the flour. Reduce the heat to low, and continue cooking for 2 to 3 minutes. Add the beef stock, and increase the heat to medium. Simmer for 15 minutes.

5. Just before you're ready to serve the soup, preheat the broiler. Ladle the soup into individual oven-safe bowls, and top each bowl with a handful of toasted bread cubes. Sprinkle a layer of cheese over top of each bowl. Place the bowls on a baking sheet, and place it under the broiler for 3 to 4 minutes or until the cheese is melted and just beginning to brown and bubble. Watch carefully, and don't leave the bowls under the broiler for too long; the cheese can burn quickly. Serve immediately. Take care; the bowls will be hot.

NOTES

If you have fresh thyme on hand, add a few sprigs with the bay leaves in step 2 and remove the stems in step 4.

You can use Monterey Jack cheese if Gruyère is hard to find.

To store, refrigerate the soup (without bread cubes or cheese) in an airtight container for up to 1 week. Reheat on the stovetop or in the microwave, and then add the bread cubes and cheese before broiling.

Turkey, Black Bean, & Sweet Potato Soup

I developed this recipe because I wanted something hearty and a little different to give to friends who were home with new babies. It may sound like a chili, but it's not. I break away from tomato-based things with this recipe and give you the part we're all looking for in a soup: meat and beans. The earthy sweetness from sweet potatoes brings it all together.

Prep time **25 minutes** • Cook time **45 minutes** • Yield **10 cups** • Serving size **2 cups**

1 tbsp extra-virgin olive oil

1 medium yellow onion, chopped

2 large carrots, chopped

3 celery stalks, chopped

1lb (450g) ground turkey

3 cloves garlic, minced

1 tbsp sweet paprika

1 tbsp granulated garlic

1 tsp ground cumin

1 tbsp kosher salt

½ tsp freshly ground black pepper

1 large sweet potato, peeled and cut into bite-sized pieces

1 (15oz; 425g) can black beans, drained and rinsed

6 cups chicken stock (for **Homemade Chicken Stock,** see page 124)

Chopped fresh cilantro (optional)

1. In a large pot, heat the oil over medium heat. Stir in the onion, carrots, and celery, and cook for 3 minutes. Add the ground turkey, and cook for 5 minutes or until browned. Stir in the minced garlic, paprika, granulated garlic, cumin, salt, and pepper. Continue cooking for 1 to 2 minutes.

2. Add the sweet potatoes and black beans, and stir until fully incorporated. Add the chicken stock, and bring to a boil. When boiling, reduce the heat to low, and simmer for at least 30 minutes. Serve topped with freshly chopped cilantro, if desired.

NOTES

Add 2 teaspoons smoked paprika for a smoky flavor profile.

Add the juice of 2 limes with the chicken stock for next-level flavor.

To store, refrigerate in an airtight container for up to 1 week.

This is a great soup to make ahead and freeze. Soup can be stored in the freezer for up to 3 months. To thaw, place the frozen soup in a pot over low heat and warm until fully heated through, or place in a slow cooker set to low for 1 to 2 hours.

Creamy Tomato Soup

Tomato soup is an American comfort-food classic, and this recipe is far better than anything you'll get out of a can. Fire-roasted tomatoes and smoked paprika give it a slightly smoky flavor that is rounded out by savory chicken stock and balanced with a pinch of sugar to cut the acidity of canned tomatoes. The addition of heavy cream creates a beautiful blush color and richness in every bite.

Prep time **25 minutes** • Cook time **45 minutes** • Yield **8 cups** • Serving size **2 cups**

3 strips bacon, chopped

1 medium yellow onion, chopped

3 cloves garlic, minced

⊕ 2 carrots, chopped

1½ tsp smoked paprika

⊕ ¼ tsp cayenne (optional)

2 tsp kosher salt

½ tsp freshly ground black pepper

1 tbsp tomato paste

1 bay leaf

⊕ 1 (28oz; 794g) can fire-roasted tomatoes with juices

1 (28oz; 794g) crushed tomatoes

1 cup chicken stock (for **Homemade Chicken Stock,** see page 124)

1 tbsp granulated sugar

⊕ 1 cup heavy cream

1. To a large pot, add the bacon and cook for 10 to 12 minutes over medium heat until crisp. Transfer the bacon to a paper towel–lined plate to drain, leaving behind about 1 tablespoon of rendered fat in the pot. Add the onion, garlic, and carrots, and cook for 3 minutes. Stir in the paprika, cayenne (if using), salt, black pepper, and tomato paste, and cook for 1 minute more. Add the bay leaf.

2. Stir in the fire-roasted and crushed tomatoes, chicken stock, and sugar, and stir until all ingredients are well combined. Reduce the heat to low, and simmer for at least 15 minutes.

3. Remove the bay leaf, and use an immersion blender to blend the soup until smooth (or to your desired consistency). If using a regular blender, do this in carefully small batches. Stir in the cream. Serve warm, topped with bacon.

NOTES
For the love of all things delicious, serve this with Parmesan Crisps (page 25) on top and a grilled cheese made with Bacon Jam (page 134) on the side. Toss in some basil ribbons if you happen to have fresh basil on hand.

To store, refrigerate in an airtight container for up to 1 week. Reheat on the stovetop or in the microwave, and add 1 to 2 tablespoons stock, milk, or water to loosen it up.

VARIATION
For a vegan version, omit the bacon and use 1 tablespoon olive oil to sauté the onion, garlic, and carrots. Replace the chicken stock with vegetable stock, and use full-fat coconut milk in place of the heavy cream.

Lemon Spaghetti
WITH GARLICKY ROASTED SHRIMP

I grew up thinking spaghetti noodles were for spaghetti with red sauce, and that was it. It wasn't until I started cooking on my own that I realized spaghetti can be tossed with just about anything. This recipe is one of my favorites because I enjoy lemon so much. Lemon brightens up any dish and pairs so well with other flavors. Succulent roasted shrimp takes this creamy, lemony pasta to the next level.

Prep time **30 minutes** • Cook time **30 minutes** • Yield **2 quarts** • Serving size **1½ cups**

- ⊕ 1lb (450g) shrimp (16/20 count), peeled and deveined
- 3 cloves garlic, minced
- ⊕ Zest and juice of 3 lemons, divided
- ⅔ cup + 1 tbsp extra-virgin olive oil
- ¼ cup + 1 tsp kosher salt, divided
- 1 tsp freshly ground black pepper, divided
- 1lb (450g) spaghetti
- 1 cup grated Parmesan cheese, plus more to garnish
- ⊕ 1 cup heavy cream
- ⊕ 1 tbsp minced fresh parsley, to garnish

1. Preheat the oven to 400°F (200°C). Line a baking sheet with foil.

2. In a large bowl, toss the shrimp with the garlic, 1 tablespoon lemon zest, 1 tablespoon olive oil, 1 teaspoon salt, and ½ teaspoon pepper. Spread the shrimp in an even layer on the prepared baking sheet. Roast for 7 to 10 minutes or until the shrimp are pink, opaque, and slightly curled. (Cooking any longer will compromise the texture of the shrimp.) Remove the shrimp from the oven and set aside.

3. While the shrimp is roasting, bring a large pot of water to a boil over high heat. When boiling, add the remaining ¼ cup salt and spaghetti. Cook for 7 minutes or until al dente. Remove from the heat, and reserve 1½ cups pasta water. Drain the pasta.

4. In a large bowl, whisk together the remaining lemon zest, lemon juice, Parmesan, and remaining ⅔ cup olive oil. Toss the pasta in the lemon mixture, adding pasta water ¼ cup at a time until the pasta is fully coated and there is a reserve of lemon sauce at the bottom of the bowl. Pour in the heavy cream, and continue tossing the pasta until the sauce has thickened slightly. Add the shrimp, and toss to coat.

5. Serve immediately, garnished with the remaining ½ teaspoon pepper, parsley, and extra Parmesan, if desired.

NOTES
For a lighter dish, omit the heavy cream.

To store, refrigerate in an airtight container for up to 1 week. Add a splash of chicken stock or water to loosen up the pasta before reheating.

VARIATION
Instead of shrimp, you could add shredded rotisserie chicken or Roasted Chicken with Root Veggies (page 69).

Pasta Carbonara

This is it: the ultimate pantry meal. A few simple ingredients—bacon, eggs, pasta, and Parmesan—converge to become a luxurious, satisfying dish. This go-to recipe is quick enough for unexpected guests but impressive enough for date night. Trust me; you'll want to have it in your arsenal.

Prep time **15 minutes** • Cook time **30 minutes** • Yield **8 cups** • Serving size **2 cups**

2 tbsp kosher salt

1lb (450g) dried pasta, spaghetti or rigatoni recommended

1 tbsp extra-virgin olive oil

4 strips bacon, chopped

4 cloves garlic, minced

⊕ ¼ tsp red pepper flakes (optional)

1 cup chicken stock (for **Homemade Chicken Stock,** see page 124)

⊕ 3 egg yolks

2 cups finely grated Parmesan cheese, divided

⊕ 3 tbsp finely chopped flat-leaf parsley

1. Bring a large pot of water to a boil. Once the water is boiling, add the salt and pasta. Cook the pasta until al dente, about 7 minutes. Remove the pot from the heat once cooked. Do not drain the pasta.

2. While the pasta is boiling, heat the olive oil in a large skillet over medium heat. Add the bacon, and cook for 10 minutes until crispy. Transfer the bacon to a paper towel–lined plate to drain, leaving the oil and rendered bacon fat in the pan.

3. Return the skillet to medium-low heat. Add the garlic and red pepper flakes, if using, and cook for 1 to 2 minutes. Add the chicken stock, and simmer for 5 to 7 minutes. The mixture should reduce by about half. Decrease the heat to low once the stock is reduced.

4. While the chicken stock is simmering, in a medium bowl, beat the egg yolks with 1 cup Parmesan cheese. While whisking vigorously, slowly add 1 cup of pasta water to the egg mixture. (This will temper the eggs, heating them gradually so they don't scramble.) Slowly add an additional 1 cup of pasta water, whisking vigorously.

5. Using tongs, transfer the cooked pasta into the skillet with the reduced chicken stock. Slowly pour in the egg mixture, and toss the pasta until it's evenly coated. Add additional pasta water, 1 cup at a time, to create more sauce if needed. The sauce will continue to thicken as it cooks over low heat. Stir in the cooked bacon, remaining 1 cup Parmesan cheese, and parsley.

NOTES

Carbonara is traditionally made with the tempered egg mixture and any extra pasta water that might be needed. If you want a creamier dish or run out of pasta water (this really shouldn't happen), you could add ¼ cup heavy cream.

To store, refrigerate in an airtight container for up to 1 week. Add a splash of chicken stock or heavy cream to loosen up the pasta before reheating.

Amazing Pantry Spaghetti

This will be the easiest and most affordable spaghetti you ever make. Gone are the days of jarred spaghetti sauce once you try this recipe. Crushed tomatoes are far more affordable and practical for your pantry. This recipe only needs a few more ingredients to bring together a quick meal.

Prep time **10 minutes** • Cook time **30 minutes** • Yield **12 cups** • Serving size **2 cups**

1 tbsp extra-virgin olive oil

1 yellow onion, diced

4 cloves garlic, minced

⊕ 1 lb (450g) ground beef or turkey

⊕ 2 tbsp Italian seasoning

4 tbsp kosher salt, divided

1 tsp freshly ground black pepper

⊕ ¼ cup tomato paste

2 tbsp balsamic vinegar

⊕ 1 tbsp anchovy paste

1 tbsp Worcestershire sauce

2 tsp granulated sugar

1 (28oz; 794g) can crushed tomatoes

3oz (85g) wedge Parmesan cheese, divided

2 bay leaves

1 lb (450g) dried spaghetti

⊕ Fresh basil, torn

1. Heat a large skillet over medium heat. Add the olive oil, and swirl to coat the skillet. Add the onion and garlic, and cook for 2 to 3 minutes until the onion is tender and slightly translucent. Add the ground beef, breaking it up into fine crumbles as it browns. Using a slotted spoon, transfer the ground beef mixture to a medium bowl. Discard the oil from the skillet. (If using ground turkey, you can skip draining the meat.)

2. Return the ground beef mixture to the pan and place over medium heat. Stir in the Italian seasoning, 1 tablespoon salt, and pepper. Cook for 1 minute. Stir in the tomato paste, balsamic vinegar, anchovy paste, Worcestershire sauce, and sugar. Pour in the crushed tomatoes. Cut the rind off the Parmesan wedge and add it to the sauce with 2 bay leaves. Reduce the heat to low, and allow the sauce to simmer for at least 15 minutes or up to 1 hour.

3. Meanwhile, bring a large pot of water to a boil. When boiling, add the remaining 3 tablespoons kosher salt. Add the spaghetti to the pot, and stir to prevent it from sticking. Cook for 7 to 8 minutes or until al dente. Drain the spaghetti, and return it to the pot.

4. Remove the Parmesan rind and bay leaves from the sauce. Carefully spoon the hot sauce into the pot with pasta. Using tongs, toss the spaghetti with the sauce until it is well coated. Gently stir in torn pieces of basil. Serve with shredded or shaved Parmesan on top.

NOTES

Garnish with a few Parmesan Crisps (page 25) and serve with the Autumn Butter Lettuce Salad (page 94).

To store, refrigerate in an airtight container for up to 1 week.

To freeze, transfer the cooled spaghetti and sauce to a freezer-safe food storage bag and place in the freezer for up to 3 months. Transfer to the refrigerator to thaw overnight before heating.

Sea Scallops
WITH BROWNED BUTTER WINE SAUCE

This is the ultimate "treat yourself" dish. The sauce is a riff on a classic *beurre blanc,* made using browned butter instead of regular butter. It becomes a tangy, slightly nutty burst of flavor that pairs perfectly with the briny taste of the scallops. Serve these scallops with Herby Risotto (page 68) for a simple but impressive meal.

Prep time **25 minutes + 4 hours to chill** • Cook time **25 minutes** • Yield **10–15 scallops** • Serving size **4–5 scallops**

8 tbsp butter

⊕ 10–15 jumbo sea scallops, about 1lb (450g)

1½ tsp kosher salt, divided

½ tsp freshly ground black pepper, divided

2 tbsp extra-virgin olive oil, divided

⊕ 1 shallot, diced

3 cloves garlic, minced

⊕ Juice of 1 lemon

⊕ ¾ cup dry white wine

⊕ 1 tbsp fresh microgreens, parsley, or chives, to garnish

1. Begin by preparing the browned butter. In a small saucepan, melt the butter over medium-low heat. Continue cooking after the foaming has subsided and the butter has stopped sizzling and crackling. Keep a watchful eye, and remove the butter from the heat when it has turned a toasty brown. This should take 10 to 12 minutes. Let the butter cool for 10 minutes, and then transfer to an airtight container and refrigerate for 4 hours or up to overnight.

2. Place the scallops on a paper towel–lined plate or baking sheet. Cover with a paper towel and press gently to remove excess liquid. Let them sit at room temperature for 20 to 30 minutes.

3. Sprinkle the scallops with ½ teaspoon salt and ¼ teaspoon pepper. Heat a large skillet over medium-high heat (a cast-iron skillet is ideal). Add 1 tablespoon oil, and gently place each scallop into the skillet, leaving ½ inch (1.25cm) of space between each scallop. (You may have to sear them in batches; use 1 tablespoon oil per batch.) Sprinkle the remaining salt and pepper on the uncooked side of each scallop. Cook the scallops for 3 to 5 minutes on each side. The scallops should have a golden-brown crust on each side. Transfer them to a plate and cover with foil to keep warm. Set aside.

4. Lower the heat to medium. To the same skillet, add the shallot and garlic, and cook in the residual oil for 1 to 2 minutes. Add the lemon juice and white wine. Cook until the liquid has reduced by half. Once the mixture is reduced, turn off the heat, and stir in the cold browned butter, one spoonful at a time, to ensure that it incorporates into the sauce. The butter should not separate.

5. Pour the sauce over the scallops, garnish with microgreens or fresh herbs, and serve immediately.

NOTE
Cold butter is vital for the success of the sauce. You can skip the browning and use regular salted butter—just make sure it's cold!

Herby Risotto

Risotto can take on many different flavors, but tossing in a variety of fresh herbs is one of the simplest and most delicious preparations. Parsley, basil, and mint complement each other well, but you can use what you like and have on hand. Do yourself a favor and serve this with Sea Scallops with Browned Butter Wine Sauce (page 67). I just gave you the perfect date-night meal. You can thank me later.

Prep time **20 minutes** • Cook time **45 minutes** • Yield **5 cups** • Serving size **1 cup**

6 cups chicken stock
(for **Homemade Chicken Stock,** see page 124)

3 tbsp butter

½ small yellow onion, finely chopped

4 cloves garlic, minced

⊕ 1½ cups Arborio rice

⊕ 1 cup dry white wine

1 cup Parmesan cheese

⊕ ½ cup chopped fresh flat-leaf parsley

⊕ ½ cup chopped fresh basil

⊕ ½ cup chopped fresh mint

2 tsp kosher salt

½ tsp freshly ground black pepper

1. In a medium saucepan, heat the chicken stock over medium heat. Allow the stock to come to a gentle simmer, and then reduce heat to medium-low to keep it warm.

2. In a large Dutch oven, melt the butter over medium heat. Add the onion and garlic, and cook for 2 to 3 minutes or until the onion is translucent. Add the rice, stirring to coat it in butter. Cook for 3 to 4 minutes. (Some of the rice will brown lightly.) Add the wine, and stir. Reduce the heat to medium-low. Cook until the wine is almost completely absorbed.

3. Add 1 cup of warm stock to the rice, stirring continuously until it is almost fully absorbed before adding another cup. Continue adding stock 1 cup at a time, stirring after each addition until the liquid is gone. Stop adding stock when the rice is fully cooked and there is a slightly thick sauce surrounding the rice. (You will likely have 1 to 2 cups of stock remaining; see note.)

4. Stir in the Parmesan cheese, parsley, basil, and mint. Season with salt and pepper, and serve immediately.

NOTES

It may seem excessive to have so much stock left over, but it's better to have extra warm stock than to heat more after you've started cooking the risotto. Leftover stock can be refrigerated in an airtight container and used for another application.

For a little extra punch, finish the risotto with freshly squeezed lemon juice.

To store, refrigerate in an airtight container for up to 1 week. Add ½ cup stock to loosen up the risotto before reheating.

Roasted Chicken
WITH ROOT VEGGIES

I consider a whole chicken a sort of blank canvas. There are so many variations of roasted chicken, and once you learn the technique, you can experiment with different seasonings. This basic recipe is packed with flavor from fresh herbs and citrus. You don't need a lot to pull off a delicious chicken dinner, and this recipe proves it.

Prep time **35 minutes** • Cook time **1 hour** • Yield **6 servings** • Serving size **1 piece chicken; ½ cup roasted veggies**

- 1 (4–6lb; 2–2.5kg) whole roasting chicken
- 1 medium yellow onion, quartered
- 2 large carrots, cut into 1-in (2.5cm) pieces
- 1 large sweet potato, cut into 1-in (2.5cm) pieces
- 1 large russet potato, cut into 1-in (2.5cm) pieces
- 6 cloves garlic
- 1½ tbsp kosher salt, divided
- 5 sprigs fresh thyme, divided
- 2 sprigs fresh rosemary, divided
- ½ cup salted butter, softened
- 1 lemon
- 1½ tsp freshly ground black pepper, divided

1. Preheat the oven to 400°F (200°C). Remove the chicken from the refrigerator, and pat dry with paper towel. Place the onion, carrots, sweet potatoes, russet potatoes, and whole garlic cloves in a large cast-iron skillet or roasting pan. Season with ½ tablespoon salt. Place 3 sprigs thyme and 1 sprig rosemary on the veggies.

2. In a medium bowl, combine the softened butter with the leaves from the remaining 2 sprigs thyme and 1 sprig rosemary. Zest the lemon, and add the lemon zest to the bowl along with ½ tablespoon salt and 1 teaspoon pepper. Stir until well combined.

3. Sprinkle the remaining ½ tablespoon salt into the cavity of the chicken. Rub the butter mixture all over the top of the chicken and under the skin. It's easiest to start under the skin then rub the outside. Be fearless! Be generous! When you feel like you've spread enough buttery love, stuff any leftover butter mixture into the cavity of the bird. Cut the zested lemon into quarters, and stuff it into the chicken cavity.

4. Place the butter-coated chicken on top of the veggies, and season with the remaining ½ teaspoon pepper. Roast for 45 to 60 minutes until the juices run clear and a meat thermometer inserted into the thickest part of the thigh reads 165°F (74°C).

5. Remove the chicken from the oven, and let it rest for at least 30 minutes before carving. Serve with the tender roasted veggies.

NOTE
To store the chicken, cut it into pieces and place it in an airtight container with the veggies. Refrigerate for up to 1 week.

VARIATION
There are many ways to adapt this recipe. Add roasted garlic instead of fresh garlic, or use additional fresh herbs such as sage, marjoram, or tarragon. Experiment with other root vegetables; parsnips, rutabaga, or turnips are all excellent.

Chicken, Mushroom, & Rice Skillet Casserole

There's nothing like a good chicken and rice casserole. My mom made it often, and there's something nostalgic about it for me. I consider this an elevated version of that childhood dish. Mushrooms are the star of this casserole. They are cooked with care to ensure they reach maximum flavor potential, leaving this dish full of umami and meaty texture.

Prep time **20 minutes** • Cook time **1 hour 30 minutes** • Yield **4 servings** • Serving size **1 chicken thigh; ½ cup rice mixture**

⊕ 4 bone-in, skin-on chicken thighs

3 tsp kosher salt, divided

2 tbsp extra-virgin olive oil, divided

⊕ 8oz (225g) white or cremini mushrooms, sliced

1 small yellow onion, diced

3 cloves garlic, minced

1 tsp granulated garlic

⊕ 1 tsp mushroom powder

1 tsp paprika

½ tsp onion powder

½ tsp freshly ground black pepper

1¼ cups long-grain white rice (see note)

2½ cups chicken stock (for **Homemade Chicken Stock,** see page 124)

Grated Parmesan cheese, to garnish

⊕ Chopped fresh chives or parsley, to garnish

1. Preheat the oven to 400°F (200°C). Pat the chicken thighs with paper towel until dry. Season the chicken on both sides using 1 teaspoon salt. Carefully rub the salt into the flesh side of the chicken thigh, allowing the salt to penetrate into the flesh.

2. Heat a large, oven-safe skillet over medium-high heat. Add 1 tablespoon oil. Place the chicken in the pan skin side down, and sear for about 5 minutes. Flip the chicken, and sear the opposite side for 3 minutes. Remove the chicken from the skillet and set aside.

3. To the same skillet, add the remaining 1 tablespoon oil and then add the mushrooms. Spread the mushrooms in an even layer in the skillet, and cook without stirring. (The mushrooms will release their liquid before browning.) After 5 minutes, toss the mushrooms around to ensure they have browned. Allow them to brown on the other side for 3 to 5 minutes.

4. When the mushrooms have fully browned, add the onion, minced garlic, granulated garlic, mushroom powder, paprika, onion powder, pepper, and remaining 2 teaspoons salt. Cook for 3 to 5 minutes. Add the rice, stirring to coat it in pan drippings and seasonings. Cook for 1 minute to allow the rice to toast lightly. Add the chicken stock, and stir until the rice is fully covered.

5. Nestle the chicken into the rice and cover with a lid. Place the chicken in the oven for 30 minutes. After 30 minutes, increase the heat to 425°F (220°C) and remove the lid. Continue to cook for 10 minutes to ensure the skin is crisp and the liquid is absorbed. Remove the skillet from the oven, and sprinkle Parmesan cheese over the top. Garnish with chives or parsley.

NOTES

If using long-grain brown rice, increase the cooking time by 15 minutes.

To store, refrigerate in an airtight container for up to 1 week. Reheat in a 400°F (200°C) oven for 5 to 7 minutes to maintain crispy skin.

Chicken 'n' Biscuit Pot Pie

If you've only had individual frozen chicken pot pies, give this recipe a try. This version replaces soggy crust with the best food in the world—biscuits. The creamy filling is loaded with veggies and tender chicken. You are not going to find this chicken pot pie in the freezer section of the grocery store.

Prep time **45 minutes** • Cook time **1 hour** • Yield **4 servings** • Serving size **1½ cups**

- 4 boneless, skinless chicken thighs
- 1 tsp extra-virgin olive oil
- 4 tsp kosher salt, divided
- 1½ tsp freshly ground black pepper, divided
- 2 tbsp butter
- 1 small yellow onion, diced
- 2 cloves garlic, minced
- 2 large carrots, diced
- 2 russet potatoes, peeled and diced
- 3 tbsp all-purpose flour
- 2 cups chicken stock (for **Homemade Chicken Stock**, see page 124)
- 3–4 sprigs of fresh thyme
- 1 bay leaf
- ½ cup frozen peas
- ½ cup heavy cream

For the biscuits
- 2 cups all-purpose flour
- ¾ tbsp baking powder
- ½ tsp baking soda
- 1 tsp kosher salt
- 1 cup heavy cream
- ½ cup + 1 tbsp butter, melted

1. Preheat oven to 400°F (200°C). Place the chicken in a 12-inch (30cm) cast-iron skillet, drizzle with olive oil, and season with 1 teaspoon salt and ½ teaspoon black pepper. Roast the chicken for 20 minutes. Carefully remove the pan from the oven, and place the chicken in a bowl to cool slightly. Shred the chicken with two forks.

2. Return the skillet to the stovetop. Melt the butter over medium heat. Add the onion, garlic, carrots, and potato. Season with the remaining 3 teaspoons salt and 1 teaspoon pepper. Sauté for 3 to 5 minutes or until tender. Sprinkle the flour over the vegetables, stir, and cook for 1 minute. Stir in the chicken stock, and whisk until the flour has dissolved. Add the thyme and bay leaf, and let the mixture come to a low boil. The mixture will begin to thicken. Reduce the heat, and simmer for 15 minutes, stirring occasionally.

3. While the filling is simmering, make the biscuits. In a medium bowl, sift together the flour, baking powder, baking soda, and salt. Stir in the heavy cream and ½ cup melted butter. The mixture will be thick and sticky.

4. Remove the thyme stems and bay leaf from the filling. Add the chicken and peas. Stir in the heavy cream, and remove the pan from the heat. Using an ice cream or cookie scoop, drop scoops of biscuit dough on top of the filling. Bake for 20 minutes or until the biscuits are browned and cooked through. Brush the remaining 1 tablespoon melted butter over the top of the cooked biscuits.

NOTES

To save time, skip step 1 and use shredded meat from a rotisserie chicken or leftover turkey. You will need about 3 cups shredded turkey or chicken.

Prepare this pot pie and freeze it before baking. Transfer the filling to an aluminum baking dish and add the biscuit dough. Wrap it tightly in plastic wrap and then with aluminum foil. It can be frozen for up to 3 months.

Chicken-Fried Steak
WITH PAN GRAVY

Cube steak is an excellent way to enjoy steak on the cheap, and chicken-fried steak is the most delicious way prepare it. Cube steak is made from top round or top sirloin that has been pounded with a meat tenderizer, which leaves a cube-like pattern on the meat. When this humble cut of meat is breaded, pan fried, and served with gravy, the result is an incredibly comforting, filling, and flavorful meal.

Prep time **35 minutes** • Cook time **30 minutes** • Yield **4 servings** • Serving size **1 steak**

4 cube steaks

1 tbsp kosher salt, divided

1 tsp freshly ground black pepper, divided

1¼ cups all-purpose flour

¼ cup cornstarch

1 tsp granulated garlic

1 tsp onion powder

½ tsp smoked paprika

¾ cup whole-milk buttermilk

1 large egg

⅓ cup canola oil

For the gravy

3 tbsp cold butter, divided

1½ cups whole milk

½ tsp kosher salt

½ tsp freshly ground black pepper

1. Season the steaks on both sides using ½ tablespoon salt and ½ teaspoon pepper. In a shallow bowl, whisk together the flour, cornstarch, granulated garlic, onion powder, paprika, remaining ½ tablespoon salt, and remaining ½ teaspoon pepper. In a second shallow bowl, whisk together the buttermilk and egg.

2. Dip one steak in the egg mixture, coating both sides. Shake off any excess, and then coat both sides of the steak with the flour mixture. Shake off any excess, and place the steak onto a baking sheet. Repeat with the remaining steaks. Do not discard the seasoning flour.

3. Allow the breaded steaks to sit at room temperature for 15 minutes. Meanwhile, preheat the oven to 250°F (120°C), and fit a baking sheet with a baking rack.

4. In a large skillet, heat the canola oil over medium-high heat. Carefully drop a pinch of flour into the oil. The flour will sizzle. If the flour does not sizzle, continue heating the oil. When the oil is hot, carefully place the steaks in the skillet and cook for 3 to 4 minutes on each side. Transfer the steaks to the prepared baking sheet, leaving space between each steak, and place them in the oven for up to 15 minutes while you make the gravy. (This is to keep the steaks warm; they are already fully cooked.)

5. In the same skillet, prepare the gravy. Discard most of the residual oil, leaving about 1 tablespoon in the pan. Add 2 tablespoons butter and ¼ cup of the reserved flour mixture to the skillet. Whisk the flour and fat together until it forms a thin paste and becomes golden brown, about 3 minutes. Slowly add the milk, and continue whisking until the flour dissolves and the milk begins to thicken. Reduce the heat to medium-low, and simmer for 5 minutes, stirring occasionally. Season with salt and pepper, and stir in the remaining 1 tablespoon butter.

6. Remove the steaks from the oven, and nestle them into the pan of gravy. Serve hot.

Competition Fried Chicken

Want to know a funny *MasterChef* story? The episode where I made perfect-looking fried chicken was also the episode where I made bland fried chicken. It looked beautiful, but I added extra flour to my dredge and forgot to increase the seasoning, too. Since then, I've made plenty of delicious fried chicken, and I've even come up with a few new tips and tricks for perfectly executed fried chicken every single time.

Prep time **15 minutes + 5 hours to marinate** • Cook time **25 minutes** • Yield **8 pieces** • Serving size **1 piece**

3 cups buttermilk

2 tbsp apple cider vinegar

½ cup hot sauce (optional; I prefer Frank's Red Hot)

2 tbsp kosher salt

1 tbsp granulated garlic

1 whole chicken, cut into 8 pieces

2 cups all-purpose flour

1 cup cornstarch

8 cups canola oil, for frying

For the seasoning blend

2 tbsp kosher salt

2 tbsp granulated garlic

2 tsp paprika

2 tsp onion powder

1 tsp ground cumin

1. In a large bowl, combine the buttermilk, vinegar, hot sauce (if using), salt, and granulated garlic. Add the chicken, turning to coat. Cover and refrigerate for at least 4 hours or overnight. Before cooking, remove the bowl from the refrigerator and let it sit at room temperature for at least 30 minutes and up to 2 hours.

2. Prepare the seasoning blend. In a small bowl, combine all ingredients.

3. In a large bowl, combine the flour, cornstarch, and half of the seasoning blend.

4. Remove the chicken from the buttermilk, and place it on a baking sheet. With the remaining seasoning blend, season the chicken pieces on both sides.

5. Dredge the chicken by coating in the flour mixture. Place the chicken on a clean baking sheet fitted with a wire rack. When all the chicken has been dredged, let it sit for 5 to 10 minutes.

6. Meanwhile, preheat the oven to 375°F (190°C). Line a baking sheet with foil and then fit with an oven-safe baking rack.

7. In a Dutch oven, heat the oil to 325°F (160°C). Carefully place 3 to 4 pieces of chicken in the hot oil. Fry for 5 to 7 minutes on each side. Do not overcrowd the pan, and remember that the breast will take the longest to fry. When the chicken is a uniform golden brown in color, remove it from the oil and place it on the prepared baking sheet.

8. When all the chicken has been fried, place the baking sheet in the oven for 20 minutes or until each piece of chicken reaches 165°F (74°C) on a meat thermometer. Test the temperature at the thickest part of the meat, close to the bone, to ensure that it's fully cooked.

NOTE
You may be tempted to use paper towels to line your baking sheet instead of a wire rack. Trust me. Get the wire rack. Placing fried chicken on a paper towel will cause it to get soggy.

Chicken & Dumplings

I consider chicken and dumplings a comforting upgrade to chicken noodle soup. Instead of noodles, the savory broth is full of tender dumplings that melt in your mouth. This tried-and-true version guarantees flavorful broth and perfectly cooked dumplings. Butter and buttermilk in the dough create a unique flavor that is rich and delicious.

Prep time **30 minutes** • Cook time **1 hour 10 minutes** • Yield **6 servings** • Serving size **2 cups**

1 tbsp extra-virgin olive oil

1 large yellow onion, diced

3 carrots, diced

4 stalks celery, diced

5 cloves garlic, diced

1 tbsp kosher salt

1 tsp freshly ground black pepper

1 whole chicken or 5–6 bone-in, skin-on thighs

4 cups chicken stock (for **Homemade Chicken Stock,** see page 124)

4 cups water

2 bay leaves

2 sprigs fresh thyme

For the dough

2 cups all-purpose flour

½ tsp baking soda

1½ tsp kosher salt

3 tbsp cold butter

¾ cup whole-milk buttermilk

1. In a large Dutch oven, heat the oil over medium heat. Add the onion, carrots, celery, and garlic. Cook for 1 to 2 minutes. Season with salt and pepper. Place the whole chicken in the pot. Add the stock and water; the chicken should be covered with liquid. Add the bay leaves and thyme. Increase the heat to high and bring to a boil. Once boiling, reduce the heat to medium-low, cover, and simmer for 1 hour.

2. Meanwhile, prepare the dough. In a large bowl, whisk together the flour, baking soda, and salt. Use a pastry cutter or two forks to cut the butter into the flour until it resembles a coarse meal. Slowly stir in the buttermilk just until everything comes together. Turn out the dough onto a floured surface and knead it lightly for about 30 seconds. Cover with a dish towel and let the dough rest while the chicken finishes cooking.

3. Using tongs, transfer the chicken to a large bowl to cool, reserving the broth in the pot. (The chicken will be tender and falling off the bone.) When cool enough to handle, remove the skin and bones from the chicken and discard. Shred the chicken into large pieces and return it to the pot. Remove the bay leaves and thyme stems. Bring the chicken and broth to a boil over medium-high heat.

4. Using your hands, gently shape the dough into a square that is about ½ inch (1.25cm) thick. Pinch off 1½-inch (4cm) pieces and drop them into the boiling broth. Once all of the dough is in the pot, reduce the heat to medium-low. Continue to simmer for 10 minutes.

NOTES

Cool to room temperature before storing. Refrigerate in an airtight container for up to 1 week.

My favorite way to eat chicken and dumplings is with a side of Fried Okra (page 109).

Fried Catfish

I have a weakness for fried fish. Crispy breading coating a tender piece of flaky fish is my go-to "safe" order at any restaurant. This recipe has a light breading made with a combination of cornmeal and flour. It is seasoned well with paprika, onion, and garlic, and it coats a piece of fish that is tenderized with buttermilk. Mustard is the secret ingredient that gives this fish a little extra flavor.

Prep time **20 minutes** • Cook time **30 minutes** • Yield **6 servings** • Serving size **1 fillet**

⊕ 1 cup buttermilk

⅓ cup yellow mustard

2 tbsp granulated garlic, divided

2 tbsp kosher salt, divided

1½ cups cornmeal

1 cup all-purpose flour

1½ tbsp smoked paprika

1 tbsp onion powder

1 tsp freshly ground black pepper

⊕ 6 catfish fillets, each 5–7oz (140–195g)

1 cup canola oil, divided, for frying

1. In a shallow bowl, whisk together the buttermilk, mustard, 1 tablespoon granulated garlic, and 1 tablespoon kosher salt.

2. In a separate shallow bowl, whisk together the cornmeal, flour, remaining 1 tablespoon granulated garlic, remaining 1 tablespoon kosher salt, smoked paprika, onion powder, and black pepper.

3. Coat one fillet on both sides with the mustard mixture. Shake off any excess, and then coat both sides of the fillet with the cornmeal mixture. Shake off any excess, and place the breaded fillet on a baking sheet. Repeat to bread the remaining fillets. Place the baking sheet in the refrigerator for 15 minutes, uncovered.

4. While the fish is resting, in a large skillet, heat ½ cup oil over medium-high heat. Add a small pinch of the breading mixture to the oil. If it bubbles upon contact with the oil, the oil is hot enough for frying. Working in batches, fry the fillets for 3 to 4 minutes per side until golden brown. Add the remaining oil in between batches, and let the oil come to temperature before frying the next batch. Transfer the fish to a paper towel–lined plate to drain. (Keep the fillets separated; otherwise, the crust will get soggy.)

NOTES

Serve Fried Catfish with Homemade Tartar Sauce (page 127) and Fresh-Cut Fries (page 98).

Allow catfish to cool completely before storing in an airtight container. Refrigerate for up to 1 week. To reheat, place on a baking sheet and warm in a 400°F (200°C) oven for 5 to 7 minutes. This will ensure the crust stays crispy.

VARIATION

This recipe can be made with any tender, white-fleshed fish, such as tilapia, swai, basa, whiting, or perch.

Cast Iron-Seared Steak
WITH GARLIC HERB COMPOUND BUTTER

I love a grilled steak, but nothing beats a juicy steak seared in cast iron. Cast iron is excellent at retaining and conducting heat and gives meat a beautiful crust. You also get to baste the steak in my favorite ingredient, butter. A compound butter with garlic, fresh herbs, and lemon zest is simple to prepare and adds amazing flavor.

Prep time **20 minutes** • Cook time **30 minutes** • Yield **4 servings** • Serving size **1 steak; 2 tbsp butter**

⊕ 4 boneless ribeye steaks, cut 1½in (4cm) thick
2 tsp kosher salt, divided
2 tbsp canola oil, divided

For the compound butter
½ cup butter, softened
1 tsp kosher salt
⊕ Zest of 1 lemon
4 cloves garlic, minced
⊕ 1 tbsp finely chopped fresh thyme
⊕ 1 tbsp finely chopped fresh parsley
⊕ 1 tbsp chopped fresh chives

1. Remove the steaks from the refrigerator at least 30 minutes before cooking, but do not exceed 2 hours out of the refrigerator. (I recommend removing them 1 hour before cooking.) Place each steak on paper towel to absorb any excess liquid.

2. Prepare the compound butter. In a small bowl, combine all ingredients and mix until thoroughly combined. Spread a long piece of plastic wrap on a work surface. Scoop the butter onto the plastic wrap in a row of heaping spoonfuls. While wrapping the butter with the plastic wrap, roll the butter to form a log shape. Place the butter in the refrigerator for at least 20 minutes.

3. Heat a 12-inch (30cm) cast-iron skillet over medium-high heat. Season 2 steaks on both sides using 1 teaspoon salt. Coat the bottom of the skillet with 1 tablespoon canola oil, and carefully place the steaks in the skillet. For medium-rare, cook on one side for 3 to 4 minutes. Flip the steaks, and cook the opposite side for 3 minutes. Add 2 tablespoons compound butter to the skillet, and baste the steaks with a spoon while cooking for 2 to 3 minutes more.

4. Remove the steaks from the skillet, and pour the remaining butter and bits on top of the steak. Let the steaks rest for 15 minutes before slicing. While resting, place 1 tablespoon compound butter on top of each steak.

5. Repeat steps 3 to 5 to cook the remaining 2 steaks using the remaining 1 teaspoon salt, 1 tablespoon canola oil, and 4 tablespoons compound butter.

VARIATION
To make blue cheese butter, add ¼ cup blue cheese crumbles to the butter mixture. (Do not use blue cheese butter to baste the steak—simply use plain butter and a couple cloves of garlic.)

Beef Stroganoff

When I got my very first apartment, I made dinner for my mom. We both love mushrooms, so I made a delicious mushroom cream sauce to go over some pasta. It wasn't until years later that I was researching recipes, and I realized I had made a sort of stroganoff for our dinner. I've honed my own recipe now, and my mom and I both love it. Now if I could just get her to make it for me!

Prep time **20 minutes** • Cook time **45 minutes** • Yield **4 servings** • Serving size **1½ cups**

- 2lb (1kg) boneless ribeye or sirloin
- 2 tsp kosher salt, divided
- 1 tsp freshly ground black pepper, divided
- 2 tbsp butter
- 2 tbsp extra-virgin olive oil
- 16oz (450g) cremini mushrooms, sliced
- 1 small yellow onion, diced
- 3 cloves garlic, minced
- 2 tbsp all-purpose flour
- 1 tbsp Dijon mustard
- 2 tsp Worcestershire sauce
- 1 tsp mushroom powder
- 2 cups beef stock
- ⅔ cup sour cream (see note)
- Long-grain white rice or egg noodles, prepared according to package directions

1. Pat the meat dry with paper towels to remove excess moisture. Thinly slice the beef, and then cut each piece in half lengthwise to create strips about 2 inches (10cm) long and ½ inch (1.25cm) thick. Season with 1 teaspoon salt and ½ teaspoon pepper.

2. In a large skillet, heat the butter and olive oil over medium-high heat. When the butter has melted, add the beef strips. Working in batches, brown the meat for 4 to 6 minutes. Transfer the cooked strips to a plate, and continue until all the beef is cooked.

3. To the same pan, add the mushrooms. Cook for 10 to 12 minutes over medium-high heat, stirring occasionally, until the mushrooms have browned on both sides and most of the liquid has evaporated.

4. Add the onion and garlic, and cook for 2 to 3 minutes. Add the flour, and cook for 1 minute, stirring to ensure the mushrooms and onion are evenly coated. Stir in the mustard, Worcestershire sauce, mushroom powder, remaining 1 teaspoon salt, and ½ teaspoon pepper. Cook for 1 minute more. Add the beef stock and beef strips, and stir to combine. Bring to a low boil, reduce the heat to low, and simmer for 15 to 20 minutes.

5. Stir in the sour cream, and cook for 5 minutes more. Serve over rice, egg noodles, or Garlic Parmesan Mashed Potatoes (page 107).

NOTES

For a creamier consistency, replace ⅓ cup sour cream with ⅓ cup cream cheese.

The stroganoff sauce can be refrigerated in an airtight container for up to 1 week. Cooked rice should be stored separately; cooked noodles can be combined with the sauce and refrigerated.

Pan-Seared Pork Chops
WITH PAN GRAVY

Pork chops can easily become dry when cooking, but an overnight brine adds flavor and moisture. The savory pan gravy also helps to keep the chops moist and is a great way to take advantage of the flavorful goodness left at the bottom of the pan.

Prep time **10 minutes** + **2 hours to marinate** • Cook time **45 minutes** • Yield **4 servings** • Serving size **1 pork chop**

⊕ 4 bone-in, center-cut pork chops, cut 1–1 ½in (2.5–4cm) thick

1 tsp granulated garlic

1 tsp onion powder

1 tsp kosher salt

½ tsp freshly ground black pepper

1 tbsp extra-virgin olive oil

For the brine

5 cups water

⅓ cup kosher salt

2 tbsp granulated sugar

5 cloves garlic

1 tbsp granulated garlic

½ tbsp onion powder

1 tbsp apple cider vinegar

5 sprigs fresh thyme

1 bay leaf

For the gravy

3 tbsp cold butter, divided

2 tbsp all-purpose flour

1 cup chicken stock (for **Homemade Chicken Stock,** see page 124)

1. In a medium saucepan, combine all of the brine ingredients. Bring to a boil over high heat. When boiling, remove from the heat, and cool to room temperature. Place the pork chops in a large bowl. Pour the cooled brine over the pork chops, ensuring that the meat is covered with liquid. Cover and refrigerate for 2 hours or up to overnight.

2. Preheat the oven to 400°F (200°C). Place a large oven-safe skillet over medium-high heat. Remove the pork chops from the brine, and pat them dry with paper towels. Season both sides of the pork chops with granulated garlic, onion powder, salt, and pepper. Add the olive oil to the hot pan, and swirl to coat. Gently place 2 pork chops in the skillet. Cook without turning for 3 to 5 minutes. Flip and cook the opposite side for 1 minute. Transfer to a plate. Cook the remaining 2 pork chops in the same skillet.

3. Return the first 2 pork chops to the skillet. (All 4 pork chops are now in the skillet.) Transfer the skillet to the oven, and cook for 10 minutes or until the meat reaches an internal temperature of 165°F (74°C). Remove the skillet from the oven, and transfer the pork chops to a plate to rest.

4. While the pork chops are resting, use the same skillet to prepare the gravy. Melt 2 tablespoons butter over medium heat. Whisk in the flour, scraping up any browned bits from the bottom of the pan. Cook for 30 seconds. While whisking, slowly pour in the chicken stock. Continue to whisk until all of the flour has dissolved. The mixture will begin to thicken. Remove the pan from the heat, and add the remaining 1 tablespoon butter to finish the gravy. Nestle the rested pork chops into the pan gravy.

VARIATION
For juicy, flavorful chicken, follow this method exactly using 4 boneless, skinless chicken breasts.

Red Beans & Rice

This is a comfort food that I crave year round, although it's especially satisfying in the winter. On a chilly day, there's nothing better than a pot of rice and beans simmering on the stove. This hearty, filling dish is packed with flavor from the smoked sausage and aromatic veggies. Although it requires a long cook time, the result is well worth it.

Prep time **30 minutes + overnight soak** • Cook time **3 hours 30 minutes** • Yield **12 cups** • Serving size **1½ cups**

1lb (450g) dry kidney beans

1 tbsp extra-virgin olive oil

1lb (450g) smoked sausage, sliced

1 large yellow onion, chopped

1 green bell pepper, chopped

3 stalks celery, chopped

4 cloves garlic, minced

1 tbsp granulated garlic

½ tbsp paprika

2 bay leaves

3 sprigs fresh thyme

3 tsp salt

1 tbsp Worcestershire sauce

10 cups chicken stock, divided (for **Homemade Chicken Stock,** see page 124)

2 cups long-grain white rice, thoroughly rinsed

1. Rinse the beans and place them in a large bowl. Add cold water to cover by at least 1 inch (2.5cm), and soak overnight. The beans will plump up, and there will be minimal water left. Drain and set aside.

2. In a large pot or Dutch oven, heat the olive oil over medium heat. Add the sausage, and cook for 5 to 7 minutes until it is brown on both sides, rendering as much fat as possible. Remove the sausage from the pot and transfer to a paper towel–lined plate to drain.

3. Add the onion, bell pepper, celery, and minced garlic to the pot. Sauté for 5 to 7 minutes or until caramelized and tender.
Add the granulated garlic, paprika, bay leaves, thyme, and salt. Cook for 2 minutes more, stirring frequently. Add the Worcestershire sauce, and cook for 1 minute more.

4. Add the beans and 6 cups chicken stock. (The liquid should come just to the top of the beans.) Bring to a boil, reduce the heat to medium-low, and cover. Simmer, covered, for 1½ hours. Remove the lid from the pot and stir. Simmer, uncovered, for 1 hour more. Remove the bay leaves and thyme stems. Using the back of a wooden spoon, mash about one-fourth of the beans against the side of the pot and continue stirring. Add the cooked sausage, and continue to cook for 30 minutes, stirring occasionally.

5. Prepare the rice during the last 30 minutes of cook time for the beans. To a medium pot, add the rice and the remaining 4 cups chicken stock. Bring to a boil, reduce the heat to low, and cover. Simmer for 25 minutes. Do not remove the lid during this time.

6. Remove the lid from the rice and fluff it with a fork to prevent it from clumping. Serve the beans over the steamed rice.

NOTES

To store, refrigerate in an airtight container for up to 5 days.

Cooled beans can be transferred to a gallon-size freezer bag and frozen for up to 3 months. To reheat, thaw in the refrigerator overnight. Heat in a pot over medium heat with 1 cup chicken stock.

Turkey Taco Skillet

This is the ultimate meal-prep recipe. It can be made early in the week and eaten over rice, quinoa, or a salad all week. I have been making this for clients for years, and it is always received well. Warm spices blended with fresh zucchini and sweet potatoes tantalize the taste buds with every bite. You'll forget it's actually a healthy meal.

Prep time **15 minutes** • Cook time **30 minutes** • Yield **6 cups** • Serving size **1½ cups**

1 tbsp extra-virgin olive oil

⊕ 1 lb (450g) ground turkey

1 small yellow onion, diced

⊕ 1 cup diced red bell pepper

⊕ 2 tbsp **Taco Seasoning** (page 135)

2 tsp granulated garlic

1 tsp smoked paprika

⊕ ½ tsp red pepper flakes (optional)

1½ tsp kosher salt

½ tsp freshly ground black pepper

1 large sweet potato, cubed

¾ cup chicken stock (for **Homemade Chicken Stock,** see page 124)

⊕ 1 medium zucchini, cubed

1. In a large skillet, heat the oil over medium heat. Add the ground turkey and cook for 5 to 8 minutes until brown, breaking up the meat with a spatula. Add the onion and bell pepper, and cook for 2 minutes. Stir in the taco seasoning, granulated garlic, paprika, red pepper flakes (if using), salt, and pepper. Cook for 1 minute.

2. Add the sweet potatoes and chicken stock. Stir to combine, scraping any browned bits from the bottom of the pan. Cover the skillet with a lid, and reduce the heat to medium-low. Cook for 12 to 15 minutes until the sweet potatoes are fork-tender.

3. Remove the lid and stir in the zucchini. Cover and cook for 5 minutes more.

NOTES

Mix with rice or quinoa, and top with Jack's Guacamole (page 23) or Pico de Salsa (page 26). It's also great in a warmed flour tortilla and eaten like a taco.

To store, refrigerate in an airtight container for up to 1 week.

VARIATION

This recipe can also be made with ground beef or chicken.

Taco Chili

Chili comes in many forms: some with beans, some without. Some are spicy, and some allow the tomatoes to shine. My chili recipe is made mostly with pantry staples and includes tender vegetables, bright tomatoes, beans, and my signature taco seasoning. Most importantly, it starts with bacon. It's a pot with a little bit of everything.

Prep time **25 minutes** • Cook time **1 hour** • Yield **10 cups** • Serving size **2 cups**

4 strips bacon, chopped

1lb (450g) ground beef

1 cup diced bell pepper (red, green, or a mix)

1 large onion, diced

4 cloves garlic, minced

3 tbsp **Taco Seasoning** (page 135)

2½ tbsp chili powder

1 tbsp granulated garlic

1 tbsp smoked paprika

1 tsp kosher salt

2 tbsp Worcestershire sauce

1 tbsp soy sauce

1 tbsp brown sugar or honey

2 bay leaves

1 (15oz; 425g) can red kidney beans, drained and rinsed

1 (15oz; 425g) can pinto beans or black beans, drained and rinsed

1 (15oz; 425g) can diced tomatoes

1 (28oz; 794g) can crushed tomatoes

1 cup beef or chicken stock

1. Heat a large Dutch oven or other heavy-bottomed pot over medium heat. Add the bacon and cook for 10 minutes or until crisp. Use a spoon to carefully remove the rendered bacon fat, leaving about 1 tablespoon of fat in the pot. (Do not remove the crispy bacon.) Add the ground beef and cook for 10 minutes, breaking up the meat until fully browned.

2. Add red and green bell peppers, onion, and minced garlic, and sauté for 2 to 3 minutes. Add the taco seasoning, chili powder, granulated garlic, paprika, and salt. Stir the mixture and allow it to cook for 1 minute. Stir in the Worcestershire sauce, soy sauce, and brown sugar. Add the bay leaves.

3. Stir in the kidney beans, pinto beans, and diced tomatoes, being careful not to break them up. Pour in the crushed tomatoes and beef stock, and stir until everything is evenly combined.

4. Reduce the heat to low. Simmer, covered, for at least 30 minutes and up to 2 hours. Remove the bay leaves before serving.

NOTES

If you don't have bacon, sauté the veggies and beef with 1 tablespoon olive oil.

Many bean varieties can be used in this chili, including light kidney beans, white beans, and navy beans.

Load up your chili with your favorite toppings, such as sour cream, shredded cheese, or scallions, and serve with Skillet Cornbread (page 93) or Hush Puppies (page 34).

To store, refrigerate in an airtight container for up to 10 days.

Chili can also be frozen in an airtight container, after being cooled completely, and stored in the freezer for up to 3 months. Reheat from frozen by placing it in a pot on low heat with ½ cup water.

Side Dishes

Flaky, Fluffy Cream Cheese Biscuits

A warm biscuit that is flaky and ever-so-slightly crisp on the outside but soft, fluffy, almost pillow-like on the inside is the ultimate comfort food. Making biscuits is therapeutic. The science of flour, tangy buttermilk, and cold fatty butter coming together is so gratifying. Biscuits are the perfect vessel for butter, and they are delicious topped with jams, jellies, honey, bacon, eggs, cheese, boneless fried chicken, and so much more.

Prep time **30 minutes** • Cook time **25 minutes** • Yield **6 biscuits** • Serving size **1 biscuit**

4 tbsp high-fat butter such as Kerrygold or Land o' Lakes European Style, frozen, plus melted butter to serve

⊕ 4 tbsp full-fat cream cheese, frozen

2 cups all-purpose flour, White Lily recommended

½ tsp baking soda

1½ tsp baking powder

1 tsp salt

⊕ ¾ cup whole-milk buttermilk

⊕ Jam or preserves (optional), to serve

1. Preheat the oven to 425°F (220°C). Line a baking sheet with parchment paper. Cut the frozen butter and cream cheese into small cubes. Place the cubes in a small bowl, and place the bowl in the freezer until ready to use.

2. In a large bowl, sift together the flour, baking soda, baking powder, and salt. Add the butter and cream cheese to the bowl. Using a pastry cutter or 2 forks, cut the butter and cream cheese into the flour mixture. The mixture should combine and come together to form pieces the size of peas. Add the buttermilk and stir with a fork.

3. Transfer the dough onto a lightly floured work surface. Gather it with your hands, working it just until it comes together into a cohesive ball. Be sure not to overmix the biscuit dough. You will end up with a tough biscuit if you work it too much.

4. Using a floured rolling pin, roll the dough into a rectangle about ¾ inch (2cm) thick. Fold the dough as you would fold a letter, bringing both ends of the dough to the middle and then folding again. Roll out the dough into a rectangle again. Repeat folding and rolling 3 more times, ending with dough rolled into a rectangle 1 to 1½ inches (2.5–3.5cm) thick. Cut the dough into squares or cut using a round biscuit cutter. (If using a round cutter, you can reroll the scraps and cut out more.) Place the biscuits on the prepared baking sheet. Bake for 20 minutes or until the tops are golden brown. Remove from the oven and brush with melted butter. Serve warm.

NOTE
To freeze, place cut, unbaked biscuits on a parchment-lined baking sheet and freeze for 1 hour and up to overnight. Once frozen, wrap each biscuit in plastic wrap and store together in a freezer-safe food storage bag. Bake according to instructions (no need to thaw).

Southern Fried Corn

This family recipe resembles the creamed corn you might find in a can, but it's so much better than anything from a supermarket shelf. My grandmother passed the recipe down to her daughter-in-law, my mom, and my mom passed it down to me. When I made it on *MasterChef,* I felt like I was showing my most authentic self on the plate. Make this for any holiday meal, and it will be devoured.

Prep time **15 minutes** • Cook time **20 minutes** • Yield **4½ cups** • Serving size **½ cup**

1 tbsp bacon fat (see note)

1 small yellow onion, chopped

2 cloves garlic, minced

4 cups fresh corn kernels cut from the cob (see note)

1 tsp kosher salt

½ tsp freshly ground black pepper

1½ cups chicken stock (for **Homemade Chicken Stock,** see page 124)

2 tbsp all-purpose flour

1 tbsp granulated sugar

¼ cup heavy cream

1. In a large sauté pan, heat the bacon fat over medium heat. Add the onion and garlic, and cook for 2 to 3 minutes until tender. Add the corn, and stir until the kernels are coated in bacon fat. Season with salt and pepper. Cover and cook for 5 to 7 minutes. The corn will begin to release a milky liquid and become tender.

2. Meanwhile, in a liquid measuring cup or small bowl, combine the chicken stock and flour to create a slurry. When the corn is tender, stir in the slurry. Let the mixture begin to bubble, and then reduce the heat to a simmer. Stir in the sugar. The mixture will start to thicken. Add the heavy cream.

3. Remove the corn from the heat when it is fully tender. The mixture will continue to thicken as it cools.

NOTES

If you don't have bacon fat, use extra-virgin olive oil. If you're looking for the added flavor of bacon fat, you can cook 2 to 3 strips of bacon and use the pan drippings. Consider chopping up the cooked bacon and adding it to the corn once the dish is done.

If fresh corn is unavailable, you can use frozen corn kernels.

To store, refrigerate in an airtight container for up to 1 week.

VARIATION

For a southwest version, sauté red and green bell pepper with the onion and garlic. Add diced jalapeño if you like it spicy!

Browned Butter Couscous Salad

That's right; I totally put "browned butter" and "salad" in the same recipe title. I am not ashamed of it at all. This salad is a little nutty, a little salty, and an absolute showstopper on the Thanksgiving table. Savory couscous is tossed with colorful roasted veggies as well as the most important ingredient in the entire world…butter!

Prep time **30 minutes** • Cook time **45 minutes** • Yield **6 cups** • Serving size **1 cup**

1 large sweet potato or 2 small sweet potatoes, cubed

2 cups quartered Brussels sprouts

½ red onion, diced

2 cloves garlic, minced

1 tbsp olive oil

1 tsp freshly ground black pepper

1½ tbsp kosher salt, divided

2 cups chicken stock (for **Homemade Chicken Stock,** see page 124)

1 cup couscous

6 tbsp salted butter

½ cup pecans, chopped

½ cup dried cranberries

½ cup crumbled feta cheese

1. Preheat the oven to 400°F (200°C). Line a baking sheet with foil.

2. In a large bowl, toss the sweet potatoes and Brussels sprouts with the onion, garlic, olive oil, pepper, and ½ tablespoon salt. Spread the vegetables evenly on the prepared baking sheet and roast for 20 to 25 minutes, tossing them halfway through to ensure that they cook evenly. When the vegetables are tender and lightly browned, remove them from the oven and set aside to cool.

3. While the veggies are roasting, in a medium saucepan, bring the chicken stock to a boil over high heat. Once boiling, stir in the couscous and the remaining 1 tablespoon salt. Cover with a lid and remove from the heat. Let the couscous sit for 4 to 5 minutes. The liquid should be fully absorbed. Remove the lid and fluff with a fork.

4. In a small saucepan, heat the butter over medium-low heat. The butter will melt and then foam, sizzling and crackling, before becoming clear. Keep a watchful eye, and remove the butter from the heat once it has turned toasty brown and smells nutty. This should take about 10 to 12 minutes. (Leaving it on the heat longer will cause the butter to burn.)

5. In a large bowl, toss the roasted vegetables with the couscous. Pour the browned butter over the mixture, and stir in the pecans, dried cranberries, and feta cheese.

NOTE
Serve warm or cold. Refrigerate leftovers in an airtight container for up to 1 week.

VARIATION
To make a browned butter pasta salad, replace the couscous with any small cooked pasta, such as elbow noodles or ditalini.

Skillet Cornbread

I don't know cornbread any way other than scratch-made and baked in a cast-iron skillet. My mom always heated the oil for the cornbread in a cast-iron skillet while she prepared the batter. Once the oil was hot, she poured it into the batter and carefully stirred it in. I was always mesmerized when she did this. Now I use the same method, but I've upgraded the ingredients, using butter instead of oil and buttermilk instead of milk.

Prep time **15 minutes** • Cook time **30 minutes** • Yield **1 10-inch (25cm) cornbread** • Serving size **8 slices**

4 tbsp butter, plus more to serve

1 cup finely ground yellow cornmeal (see note)

1 cup all-purpose flour (see note)

½ tsp baking soda

½ tsp baking powder

¼ tsp salt

⅔ cup granulated sugar

⊕ 2 eggs

⊕ 1 cup whole-milk buttermilk

Honey (optional), to serve

1. Place the butter in a 10-inch (25cm) cast-iron skillet. Place the skillet in a cold oven, and preheat the oven to 350°F (175°C). (The butter will melt as the oven preheats.)

2. Meanwhile, in a large bowl, combine the cornmeal, flour, baking soda, baking powder, salt, and sugar. In a medium bowl, beat the eggs and buttermilk together, making sure the eggs are thoroughly beaten. Add the wet ingredients to the dry ingredients and stir to combine.

3. Remove the skillet from the oven, and carefully pour the melted butter into the cornbread batter. Gently stir the butter into the batter until it is fully incorporated. Scrape the batter into the hot skillet. (Be careful not to burn yourself on the skillet). Return the skillet to the oven to bake for 30 to 40 minutes or until the cornbread is golden brown and a toothpick inserted into the center comes out clean. Cool for a minimum of 15 minutes before cutting. Serve with butter and honey, if desired.

NOTES
You will achieve next-level fluffiness if you use White Lily cornmeal and flour. Or make this with White Lily self-rising flour and self-rising buttermilk cornmeal, and omit the baking soda and baking powder.

I recommend using whole-milk buttermilk, but low-fat buttermilk is sufficient if that's all you can find.

If you don't have a cast-iron skillet, you can use an 8 × 8-inch (20 × 20cm) or 9 × 9-inch (23 × 23cm) glass baking dish.

VARIATION
Consider adding shredded cheese and a can of diced jalapeños to the batter for a spicy cornbread that will pair perfectly with Taco Chili (page 85).

Autumn Butter Lettuce Salad

This salad is a beautiful surprise of tender lettuce, sweet fennel, and hearty radicchio, tossed with a simple vinaigrette made with pantry staples. The fresh apple adds a bright flavor and crisp texture, and the sunflower seeds bring everything together with a little saltiness and crunch.

Prep time **20 minutes** • Cook time **none** • Yield **4–5 cups** • Serving size **1 cup**

- 1 large head of butter lettuce
- 1 head of radicchio
- 1 bulb fennel
- 1 Honeycrisp apple
- ¼ cup **Apple Cider Vinaigrette** (page 122)
- ¼ cup roasted, salted sunflower seeds
- 1 (4oz; 115g) wedge Parmesan cheese

1. Remove any bruised leaves from the butter lettuce and radicchio. Leaving the stems intact, cut the heads of lettuce into thick strips. Discard the stems. Place the lettuce and radicchio in a large bowl.

2. To prepare the fennel, cut off the stalks and the bottom stem. Cut the bulb in half lengthwise and then into quarters. Remove any bruised or wilted outer layers. Thinly slice each fennel quarter crosswise from the top to the root. Add the fennel to the bowl.

3. Core the apple and cut into quarters. Thinly slice each quarter lengthwise. Cut the slices into matchsticks. Add the apples to the bowl, and gently toss the lettuce blend, fennel, and apple with the vinaigrette. Toss in the sunflower seeds.

4. Turn the salad onto a large platter and use a vegetable peeler to create large shavings of Parmesan cheese over the top of the salad.

NOTE
The vegetables and apples can be prepped and refrigerated in a large bowl covered with plastic wrap for several hours in advance. Toss the salad with the vinaigrette, and finish with the sunflower seeds and Parmesan right before serving.

Mom's Corn on the Cob

In this simple recipe, fresh sweet corn is slowly simmered to bring out its natural sweetness, resulting in a supremely satisfying side dish that is remarkably buttery and tender. My mom started making corn on the cob this way because my dad wouldn't leave her any room on the grill for the corn. She often makes it in the summer, when corn is plentiful in Indiana. It is the best corn on the cob I've ever had.

Prep time **15 minutes** • Cook time **35 minutes** • Yield **6–8 ears of corn** • Serving size **1 ear of corn**

⊕ 6–8 ears fresh sweet corn, shucked (see note)

2 tbsp kosher salt

3 tbsp granulated sugar

½ cup butter, plus more for serving

1. Rinse each ear of corn in water and check to make sure all the corn silk has been removed. To a large stockpot, add the corn and enough water to cover by 1 inch (2.5cm). Bring to a boil over high heat. Once boiling, add the salt, and reduce the heat to medium. Cover with a lid, and simmer for 20 minutes.

2. Remove the lid and add the sugar and butter. Cover and cook for 15 minutes more.

3. Remove the pot from the heat, and allow the corn to sit in the buttery water until ready to serve. Serve warm with an extra pat of butter to melt over the corn.

NOTES

You can cut the ears of corn in half or leave them whole.

If fresh sweet corn is unavailable, you can use frozen corn on the cob. Add it when frozen; do not thaw it before cooking.

Remove the corn from the cooking liquid for storage. Refrigerate in an airtight container or food storage bag for up to 1 week.

Collard Green & Sweet Potato Salad

The misconception about collard greens is that they can only be simmered down with some sort of smoked protein to taste good. That is the farthest thing from the truth. Collard greens are incredibly versatile and pair well with a lot of different flavors. The key to delicious collard greens is knowing how to clean them, treat them, and pair them with the best flavors. This salad does precisely that.

Prep time **30 minutes** • Cook time **20 minutes** • Yield **8 cups** • Serving size **1½ cups**

2 large sweet potatoes, peeled and cubed

2 tbsp extra-virgin olive oil, divided

1 clove garlic, minced

1 tsp paprika

1 tsp granulated garlic

2 tsp kosher salt, divided

½ tsp freshly ground black pepper

⊕ ½ cup pecan halves

⊕ 1 bunch of collard greens (about 1lb; 450g), ribs removed and leaves thoroughly cleaned

⊕ ⅓ cup **Warm Bacon Dressing** (page 123)

1 small red onion, thinly sliced

⊕ ½ cup shaved Parmesan cheese

1. Preheat the oven to 400°F (200°C). Line a baking sheet with foil.

2. In a large bowl, toss the sweet potatoes with ½ tablespoon olive oil, minced garlic, paprika, granulated garlic, 1 teaspoon salt, and pepper. Spread the sweet potatoes evenly on the prepared baking sheet, and bake for 15 to 20 minutes or until fork-tender. Set aside to cool.

3. In a small, dry skillet, toast the pecans over medium-low heat for 3 to 5 minutes, watching closely to be sure that they don't burn. Remove from the heat and cool before chopping.

4. While the sweet potatoes are cooling, stack several collard green leaves and roll them tightly like a cigar. Slice widthwise at regular intervals down the roll to form thick shreds. Repeat until all the leaves are shredded. Place the shredded collard greens in a large bowl, and add the remaining 1½ tablespoons olive oil and 1 teaspoon salt. Using your hands, gently massage the greens, and then toss them with the warm bacon dressing.

5. To assemble, top the dressed greens with the roasted sweet potatoes, onion, Parmesan, and pecans. Serve with extra dressing on the side.

VARIATION
This salad can be served with goat cheese or feta cheese instead of Parmesan. You can also use toasted pistachios or sliced toasted almonds instead of pecans.

Fresh-Cut Fries

I am a self-proclaimed French fry connoisseur. Whenever I'm not sure what I want to eat, I opt for French fries. These fries are cooked twice to ensure they are crispy on the outside and soft on the inside. Salting them immediately after they come out of the hot oil makes the potato flavor shine. You will not make any other fry once you start making these.

Prep time   **15 minutes** • Cook time   **40 minutes** • Yield   **4 heaping cups** • Serving size   **1 heaping cup**

2 large russet potatoes, rinsed and patted dry

2qt (2l) canola or vegetable oil, for frying

Kosher salt, sea salt, or flaky sea salt

1. In in a large Dutch oven or other heavy-bottomed pot, heat the oil to 325°F (160°C). (Use a candy thermometer to measure the oil temperature.) While the oil is heating, cut the potatoes into sticks about ¼ inch (.5cm) thick. It's okay to leave the skin on!

2. When the oil has come to temperature, slowly add about one-fourth of the potatoes to the pot. Be careful not to splatter yourself with hot oil. Add the potatoes slowly, low in the pot, and lay them away from you. Fry for 3 to 4 minutes. Before they begin to turn brown, remove the potatoes using tongs or a kitchen spider, and place on a paper towel–lined baking sheet. Be careful to keep the fries from touching while cooling on the baking sheet. Fry the remaining raw potatoes. Allow the potatoes to cool uncovered at room temperature.

3. Once the fries have come to room temperature, heat the same pot of oil to 350°F (175°C). Working in batches, add the par-cooked fries back to the oil and fry until golden brown, about 5 to 7 minutes per batch. Remove them from the oil and place them on a fresh paper towel–lined baking sheet. Immediately season with salt and serve.

NOTES
For extra-crispy fries, cook for an additional 1 to 2 minutes during the second fry.

To reheat, spread on a baking sheet and place in a 400°F (200°C) oven for 5 to 7 minutes.

Don't forget the condiments! Serve with Sweet Onion Ketchup (page 131), Homemade Mayo (page 126; try adding a little sriracha!), or Parmesan Ranch (page 126).

VARIATION
Spice things up by sprinkling the fries with Savory Dry Rub (page 135) or Taco Seasoning (page 135) right after frying.

Church Lady Potato Salad

Potato salad is always on the menu at a church BBQ, but only certain church ladies are allowed to make it. While I don't consider myself a church lady, I do consider myself a good potato salad maker. I got my skills from the ultimate church ladies, my mom and Sister Powell. Tangy vinegar, mustard, and dill are balanced by the sweetness of honey and sweet salad cubes. Celery and onion provide a light crunch.

Prep time **30 minutes** • Cook time **15 minutes** • Yield **8 cups** • Serving size **½ cup**

4 large russet potatoes, peeled and cut into 1-in (2.5cm) cubes

⊕ 4 eggs

3 tbsp kosher salt

½ small red onion, diced

⊕ 2 stalks celery, diced

1 tsp smoked paprika

For the dressing

⊕ ¾ cup mayonnaise (for **Homemade Mayo**, see page 126)

⊕ ¼ cup sweet salad cubes or sweet pickle relish

2 tbsp yellow mustard

2 tbsp honey

1 tbsp red wine vinegar

1½ tsp granulated garlic

1 tsp onion powder

⊕ ½ tsp celery salt

½ tsp kosher salt

1 tsp smoked paprika

½ tsp freshly ground black pepper

1. To a large pot, add the potatoes and enough water to cover by 1 inch (2.5cm). Gently nestle the uncooked eggs into the potatoes. Place the pot over high heat and lay a wooden spoon across the top of the pot. (This will prevent the potatoes from boiling over.) Once the water is boiling, add 3 tablespoons salt. Allow the potatoes and eggs to boil for 12 to 15 minutes. The potatoes are done when they are fork-tender. Be careful not to overcook the potatoes.

2. Meanwhile, prepare an ice bath by filling a medium bowl with water and ice. When the potatoes are done, use a slotted spoon to remove the eggs from the pot and gently place them in the ice bath to cool. Drain the potatoes using a colander. Transfer the potatoes to a large bowl and set aside.

3. While the eggs are cooling, prepare the dressing. In a medium bowl, whisk together all dressing ingredients.

4. Peel the eggs, and rinse them to remove any residual bits of shell. Chop the eggs, and add them to the bowl with the potatoes. Add the onion and celery. Pour the dressing over top, and gently toss until the potatoes are evenly coated. Be careful not to overmix the potatoes. Sprinkle 1 teaspoon paprika over the top of the potato salad. Cover with plastic wrap, and refrigerate for 2 hours and up to overnight.

NOTES

Potato salad can be made ahead of time and served cold or room temperature. Do not allow the potato salad to sit at room temperature for more than 2 hours.

To store, refrigerate in an airtight container for up to 1 week.

Smoky Spiced Roasted Cauliflower

Cauliflower has a very distinct flavor, and it's not rice. Can we all agree on that? While I don't like cauliflower rice, I do appreciate how cauliflower can take on other flavors. This smoky cauliflower has a beautiful medley of spices that tells the cauliflower who's boss while playing nice. I love it so much that I've even made it for a quick snack.

Prep time **20 minutes** • Cook time **15 minutes** • Yield **4 cups** • Serving size **1 cup**

- 1 large head cauliflower, cut into florets
- 1 tbsp extra-virgin olive oil
- 2 tsp granulated garlic
- 2 tsp smoked paprika
- 1 tsp onion powder
- ¼ tsp red pepper flakes
- ½ tsp ground turmeric
- 1 tsp kosher salt
- ½ tsp freshly ground black pepper

1. Preheat the oven to 400°F (200°C). Line a baking sheet with foil.

2. Place the cauliflower in a large bowl. Drizzle the olive oil over the cauliflower, and sprinkle on each of the remaining ingredients. Toss until each piece of cauliflower is coated in seasonings.

3. Spread the cauliflower evenly on the prepared baking sheet, and roast for 15 to 20 minutes. The cauliflower should be tender but firm. (Cook for 5 minutes more if you prefer more tender cauliflower.)

NOTES

This recipe is excellent as a side dish, but it's also fantastic as a topping for salad. It's delicious hot, at room temperature, and even cold.

To store, refrigerate in an airtight container for up to 1 week.

Slow-Cooked Black-Eyed Peas

There is a beautiful history around black-eyed peas and how they are connected to Black culture. A prominent legume planted by enslaved people, black-eyed peas provide a wealth of nitrogen to the soil. They are now considered a symbol of prosperity and freedom and are often eaten on New Year's Day. These black-eyed peas are savory, creamy, and comforting. Their briny flavor pairs perfectly with a hunk of cornbread or fried chicken.

Prep time **30 minutes + overnight soak** • Cook time **3 hours 30 minutes** • Yield **10 cups** • Serving size **1 cup**

1lb (450g) dried black-eyed peas

3 tbsp kosher salt, divided

6 strips thick-cut bacon, chopped

1 large yellow onion, diced

4 cloves garlic, minced

1 tsp smoked paprika

1 tsp granulated garlic

½ tsp freshly ground black pepper

⊕ 2 smoked ham hocks

2 bay leaves

⊕ 4 sprigs fresh thyme

8 cups chicken stock (for **Homemade Chicken Stock,** see page 124)

1. Pour the dried beans into a large bowl. Discard any stones or discolored beans. Add water to cover the beans by about 5 inches (13cm). Add 2½ tablespoons salt, and stir until the salt has dissolved. Cover the bowl with a plate or dish towel and let soak overnight.

2. Heat a large Dutch oven over medium heat. Add the bacon, and cook for 12 to 15 minutes until crisp. Add the onion, and cook for 2 to 3 minutes until the onion is tender. Add the minced garlic, and cook for 1 minute more. Add the remaining ½ tablespoon salt, paprika, granulated garlic, and pepper. Stir to distribute the seasonings evenly.

3. Add the ham hocks, bay leaves, and thyme, and toss around until they are coated in the residual oil. Add the chicken stock, cover, and reduce the heat to medium-low. Simmer for 1 hour. The meat of the ham hocks should be fork-tender and pulling away from the bone.

4. Drain the black-eyed peas in a colander, and carefully add them to the pot. Stir to ensure they are fully incorporated, and return the lid to the pot. Simmer over medium-low heat for 1 hour.

5. Remove the lid and stir. Cook uncovered for 30 minutes more. The liquid should reduce by about half. Remove the bay leaves and thyme stems. Use a wooden spoon to mash about 1 cup of beans against the inside of the pot. This will create a gravy. Stir the gravy into the remaining liquid and cook for 20 to 30 minutes more.

NOTES

Enjoy these with a slice of Skillet Cornbread (page 93) while sitting in comfy sweats under a blanket.

To store, refrigerate in an airtight container for up to 1 week.

VARIATION

If you don't have black-eyed peas, the same method can be used to prepare slow-cooked pinto beans or navy beans.

Dad's Baked Beans

My dad's baked beans are the only ones I'll eat. Grating the green bell pepper makes them unique; you get a hint of bell pepper flavor without actual pieces of pepper. The beans are baked with strips of bacon on top, so all that smoky bacon flavor can seep down into the beans, making them extra decadent and delicious.

Prep time **25 minutes** • Cook time **1 hour** • Yield **6 cups** • Serving size **1 cup**

4 strips of bacon, divided

1 yellow onion, diced

⊕ ½ green bell pepper, grated

4 cloves garlic, minced

1 tsp granulated garlic

1 tsp paprika

1 tsp onion powder

2 tsp kosher salt

½ tsp freshly ground black pepper

1 tbsp Worcestershire sauce

⊕ ¼ cup molasses or honey

⅔ cup brown sugar

⊕ 1 cup ketchup

1 (15oz; 425g) can navy beans, drained and rinsed

1 (15oz; 425g) can Great Northern beans, drained and rinsed

1 (15oz; 425g) can pinto beans, drained and rinsed

1. Preheat the oven to 350°F (175°C).

2. Heat a medium pot over medium heat. Chop 2 strips of bacon, and add to the pot. Cook for 8 to 10 minutes until crisp. Remove the bacon with a spoon, leaving behind about 1 tablespoon of rendered bacon fat. Set the bacon aside.

3. To the pot, add the onion, bell pepper, and minced garlic. Cook for 2 to 3 minutes until the onion is tender and slightly translucent. Stir in the granulated garlic, paprika, onion powder, salt, and pepper. Cook for 1 minute more. Add the Worcestershire sauce, molasses, and brown sugar, and stir until evenly distributed. Add the ketchup, and stir until the brown sugar has dissolved. Add the beans and the cooked bacon pieces, and stir until evenly coated.

4. Carefully transfer the hot beans to a 9 × 13-in (23 × 33cm) baking dish. Place the remaining 2 strips of bacon over the top of the beans. Bake for 45 minutes to 1 hour. The beans should be saucy but firm, and the bacon should be fully cooked through.

NOTES

Baked beans can be prepared ahead, covered in plastic wrap, and refrigerated until ready to bake. Allow the baking dish to come to room temperature before baking.

To store, cover the baking dish with aluminum foil or plastic wrap and refrigerate for up to 1 week.

VARIATION

Although this recipe calls for three different varieties of beans, you can use just about any beans you have on hand.

Make this meatless by leaving out the bacon and sautéing the veggies in 1 tablespoon extra-virgin olive oil. Be sure to use smoked paprika if you leave out the bacon.

Mom's Mac & Cheese

My mom, Frankie Askew, has received a standing ovation for her mac and cheese. It's just that good. Of course, I had to be super extra and put my own spin on things, but my mom deserves all the credit for this recipe. The cream cheese is what sets it apart. It's not melted into the cheese sauce base. Instead, it's highlighted throughout the oozy baked goodness. Round of applause for my mom, ya'll.

Prep time **15 minutes** • Cook time **1 hour** • Yield **1 9 × 13-inch (23 × 33cm) casserole** • Serving size **1 cup**

3½ tbsp salt, divided

1lb (450g) elbow macaroni

6 tbsp butter, cut into cubes, divided

⊕ 8oz (225g) cream cheese, cut into cubes

⊕ 4½ cups shredded sharp cheddar cheese, divided

⊕ 3 cups shredded medium cheddar cheese, divided

¼ cup all-purpose flour

⊕ 4 cups whole milk, divided

⊕ 2 eggs

1 tbsp granulated garlic

1 tsp paprika

1 tbsp Worcestershire sauce

1. Preheat the oven to 350°F (175°C). Bring a large pot of water to a boil over high heat. When boiling, add 3 tablespoons salt, and stir in the macaroni. Cook for 7 minutes or until al dente, and drain.

2. To a 9 × 13-inch (23 × 33cm) baking dish, add the cooked macaroni and 4 tablespoons cubed butter. Stir until the butter has melted and coats the macaroni. Add the cream cheese, 2 cups sharp cheddar, and 2 cups medium cheddar, and toss with the macaroni. The goal is not to melt the cheese; you want to keep some shape to the cubes and cheese shreds. Set aside.

3. In a medium saucepan, melt the remaining 2 tablespoons butter over medium heat. Add the flour, and whisk to combine the flour and butter until all the clumps are gone and the mixture is smooth. Cook for 1 minute more. Slowly drizzle in 1 cup milk, and whisk until fully incorporated. Increase the heat to medium-high and bring the mixture to a low simmer. Continue to cook, whisking every 1 to 2 minutes, until the mixture begins to thicken. Add the remaining 3 cups milk and allow the mixture to continue cooking and thickening for another 2 minutes. Reduce the heat to low.

4. In a small bowl, beat the eggs. To temper the eggs, add about ½ cup of the hot sauce to the eggs and whisk briskly to combine. Whisk in another ½ cup of the sauce, and then pour the egg mixture back into the pan with the remaining sauce.

5. Slowly whisk in 1 cup sharp cheddar and 1 cup medium cheddar, adding a small handful at a time and whisking until the cheese is fully incorporated. Stir in the granulated garlic, paprika, Worcestershire, and remaining ½ tablespoon salt.

6. Slowly pour the cheese sauce into the baking dish and combine with the macaroni mixture. Spread the macaroni mixture evenly in the baking dish, and top with the remaining 1½ cups shredded sharp cheddar. Bake for 35 to 40 minutes. The cheese on top should be bubbly, and the edges should be slightly browned.

Maple-Bourbon Mashed Sweet Potatoes

This is one of the side dishes I made for my *MasterChef* audition. I was so proud of this dish because it is unique and packed with flavor. Although this recipe pairs sweet potatoes with maple syrup and bourbon, it is not overly sweet. Serve these sweet potatoes alongside the Pan-Seared Pork Chops with Pan Gravy (page 81) for a meal that will impress even the toughest judges.

Prep time **15 minutes** • Cook time **35 minutes** • Yield **5 cups** • Serving size **1 cup**

3–4 large sweet potatoes, peeled and quartered

1½ tbsp kosher salt, divided

4 tbsp butter, cut into cubes

⊕ ¾ cup heavy cream

½ tsp freshly ground black pepper

⊕ 3 tbsp maple syrup or honey

⊕ 2 tsp bourbon

1. To a large pot, add the sweet potatoes and enough water to cover by about 1 inch (2.5cm). Bring to a boil over high heat. (Place a wooden spoon across the top of the pot to prevent the potatoes from boiling over.) When boiling, add ½ tablespoon salt. Cook for 12 to 15 minutes or until the potatoes are fork-tender.

2. Carefully drain the hot potatoes using a colander. Return the potatoes to the pot, and place the potatoes back on the same heating element on which they were cooked. Make sure the heat is off. (This will allow the residual heat to dry any excess moisture from the pot and the potatoes.) Add the cubed butter, and use a potato masher to begin mashing the potatoes. While mashing, carefully add the heavy cream ¼ cup at a time. Stir in the remaining 1 tablespoon salt along with the pepper, maple syrup, and bourbon. Serve warm.

NOTES

Mashed sweet potatoes can be made early in the day and served later. To keep the mashed sweet potatoes warm, place them in a heat-safe bowl and cover with plastic wrap. Place the bowl inside a simmering pot of water or in a slow cooker on the Warm setting.

To store, refrigerate in an airtight container for up to 1 week.

VARIATION

For a dairy-free version, use ¾ cup canned coconut milk, including the solids that rise to the top of the can, in place of the butter and heavy cream.

Garlic Parmesan Mashed Potatoes

I consider myself one of the best mashed potato makers ever. Every time I make this version with roasted garlic and Parmesan, I show myself a little appreciation by doing a little dance in the kitchen. These decadent mashed potatoes are outrageously flavorful and worthy of any dinner table, whether it's an average Tuesday evening or a Christmas feast. Give them a try—and don't forget to do a little dance for yourself when you're done.

Prep time **15 minutes** • Cook time **45 minutes** • Yield **8 cups** • Serving size **1 cup**

For the roasted garlic
1 large bulb garlic
½ tsp extra-virgin olive oil
½ tsp kosher salt

For the potatoes
4 large russet potatoes
1½ tbsp kosher salt, divided
⊕ 1¼ cups heavy cream
⊕ 3 sprigs fresh thyme
4 tbsp cold butter, cubed
1 tsp freshly ground black pepper
1 cup shredded Parmesan cheese or cheddar cheese
⊕ 2 tbsp minced fresh chives or parsley

1. Preheat the oven to 400°F (200°C). Cut the garlic bulb in half through the equator. Drizzle the cut side of each half with oil and sprinkle with salt. Place the two halves together, and wrap the bulb tightly with foil. Place on a baking sheet, and roast for 25 to 30 minutes until tender and lightly browned. Set aside to cool.

2. Meanwhile, peel the potatoes and cut them into quarters. Place them in a large pot, and add water to cover by about 1 inch (2.5cm). Bring the pot to a boil over high heat. (Place a wooden spoon across the top of the pot to prevent the potatoes from boiling over.) When boiling, add ½ tablespoon salt. Cook for 12 to 15 minutes or until the potatoes are fork-tender. Take care not to overcook the potatoes.

3. Meanwhile, to a small saucepan, add the heavy cream and thyme. Bring to a gentle simmer over medium heat. Reduce the heat to low and let the thyme steep until it is time to mash the potatoes.

4. Carefully drain the hot potatoes using a colander. Return the potatoes to the pot, and place the potatoes back on the same heating element on which they were cooked. Make sure the heat is off. (This will allow the residual heat to dry any excess moisture from the pot and the potatoes.) Add the cubed butter, and squeeze the roasted garlic into the potatoes. Using a potato masher, begin mashing the potatoes. While mashing, carefully add the warm heavy cream ½ cup at a time. Season the potatoes with the remaining 1 tablespoon salt and the pepper. Fold in the Parmesan cheese and chives. Serve warm.

NOTES
Mashed potatoes can be made early in the day and served later. To keep the mashed potatoes warm, place them in a heat-safe bowl and cover with plastic wrap. Place the bowl inside a simmering pot of water or in a slow cooker on the Warm setting.

To store, refrigerate in an airtight container for up to 1 week.

Fried Okra

Okra is my favorite vegetable in the whole wide world. Hand downs. Not up for debate. This fried okra has a light, crisp coating thanks to the cornstarch. It's a little addition I made when stealing my grandmother's recipe. Grandma Lillie used to make fried okra all the time; it is one of the fondest memories I have of her. I genuinely hope you love this recipe as much as I do.

Prep time **20 minutes** • Cook time **30 minutes** • Yield **2 cups** • Serving size **½ cup**

4 cups canola oil, for frying

1 cup cornmeal

1 cup all-purpose flour

¼ cup cornstarch

⊕ 2 tbsp Creole seasoning blend (see note)

⊕ 1½ cups sliced fresh okra, cut into ¼-in (.5cm) slices

⊕ ¾ cup whole-milk buttermilk

Kosher salt

1. In a large pot, heat the canola oil over medium-high heat to 350°F (175°C).

2. In a large bowl, whisk together the cornmeal, flour, cornstarch, and Creole seasoning. Set aside.

3. To a medium bowl, add the okra and buttermilk. Let the okra soak for 1 minute. Drain the okra slightly by pouring it into a colander. Do not shake the colander; there should be some excess buttermilk clinging to the okra.

4. Coat about ½ cup of the drained okra with the cornmeal mixture. Use your fingers or a fine mesh sieve to shake off the excess cornmeal. Add the breaded okra to the hot oil.

5. Cook the okra for about 3 to 4 minutes or until it becomes a deep golden brown on all sides. Remove it from the oil using a slotted spoon or a kitchen spider, and place it on a paper towel–lined plate. Season immediately with salt. Continue cooking okra in batches until all of it has been fried. Serve immediately.

NOTES

I recommend Tony Chachere's Creole seasoning. If using a salt-free Creole seasoning blend, add ½ teaspoon salt.

This recipe is best with fresh okra, but it can be hard to find year-round. If you get a hankering for fried okra outside of the summer months, you can make this with frozen sliced okra. (Skip the buttermilk soak if using frozen okra.)

Braised Greens

This recipe was born out of necessity. I wanted to make something that captured the flavor of my mom's slow-cooked collard greens, but could be made in a fraction of the time. Swapping out tougher collards for more tender Swiss chard cuts down on the cook time and results in greens that are tender and savory from plenty of garlic. Maple syrup lends a little sweetness to cut the bitterness of the greens.

Prep time **30 minutes** • Cook time **20 minutes** • Yield **2 cups** • Serving size **½ cup**

- ⊕ 2 bunches of rainbow Swiss chard
- 1 tsp extra-virgin olive oil
- 3 cloves garlic, minced
- ¼ cup chicken stock (for **Homemade Chicken Stock,** see page 124)
- ⊕ Juice of ½ lemon or 2 tsp apple cider vinegar
- 2 tsp kosher salt
- ½ tsp freshly ground black pepper
- ⊕ ½ tsp maple syrup or honey

1. Wash the chard thoroughly to remove any dirt. Trim the stems. Remove the leaves from the stems, and chop or tear the leaves into bite-sized pieces. Cut the stems in half lengthwise and finely chop. Keep the chopped leaves and stems separate.

2. In a large skillet, heat the oil over medium-low heat. Add the garlic, and cook for 1 minute. (Do not increase the heat; high heat will cause the garlic to burn quickly.) Add the chard stems and cook for 2 to 3 minutes. The stems should become tender and slightly translucent.

3. Add the greens to the pan, and toss until thoroughly coated in garlic and oil. You may have to add the greens in batches, waiting for 1 to 2 minutes between each addition for the greens to wilt, making room to add more. Continue until all of the greens have been added to the skillet.

4. Add the chicken stock, and cook for 3 to 5 minutes. Once the greens are fully wilted, add the lemon juice, and season with salt and pepper. Cook for 3 to 5 minutes more, uncovered, to allow the liquid to concentrate a bit. To finish, drizzle the maple syrup over the greens and toss until evenly distributed. Serve hot.

NOTE
Swiss chard stems should not be discarded; when finely chopped, they give a celery-like texture to the greens. However, if you choose to make this recipe with tougher greens like kale, collard greens, or dandelion greens, you will want to discard the stems.

Garlicky Green Beans

For me, sautéed green beans bring to mind the super-bland side dish served at most catered affairs. It's a straightforward and convenient way to cook green beans for the masses, but they just aren't tasty. This recipe has all the convenience of sautéed green beans, but a generous amount of garlic and savory chicken stock make this dish as flavorful as the slow-cooked green beans my grandma used to make.

Prep time **15 minutes** • Cook time **15 minutes** • Yield **3 cups** • Serving size **¾ cup**

1 tsp extra-virgin olive oil

5 cloves garlic, minced

⊕ 1½lb (680g) fresh green beans, trimmed

1½ tsp kosher salt

½ tsp freshly ground black pepper

⊕ ¾ cup chicken stock (for **Homemade Chicken Stock,** see page 124)

1. In a large skillet, heat the olive oil over medium-low heat. Add the garlic, and cook for 1 minute, ensuring the garlic doesn't burn. Add the green beans, and toss until fully coated in oil. Cook for 1 to 2 minutes.

2. Season the green beans with salt and pepper. Add the chicken stock, and increase the heat to medium-high. Cook until the liquid has reduced by half.

3. Green beans are done when they are tender and fully coated in chicken stock.

NOTES

Use bacon fat instead of olive oil if you have it.

I do not recommend using canned or frozen green beans. Too much water is retained in both types of green beans, which will lead to a bland and soggy result.

VARIATION

Top with toasted sliced almonds if you want a textural crunch.

Bacon Balsamic Brussels Sprouts

Brussels sprouts have become a favorite vegetable for a whole generation of people who grew up hating them as kids. Of course, we take them to the next level by deep-frying them or cooking them with bacon, and leave the boiled method to our mothers. I was one of those kids who didn't like Brussels sprouts, but now I can't get enough. These bacon balsamic Brussels sprouts are no exception. They are deliciously salty and perfectly sweet.

Prep time **5 minutes** • Cook time **25 minutes** • Yield **2 cups** • Serving size **½ cup**

4 strips thick-cut bacon, chopped

⊕ 1 lb (450g) Brussels sprouts, trimmed and quartered

2 cloves garlic, minced

1 tsp kosher salt

½ tsp freshly ground black pepper

¼ cup balsamic vinegar

2 tbsp honey

1. Preheat the oven to 400°F (200°C). Line a baking sheet with foil.

2. Spread the bacon evenly on the prepared baking sheet. Place in the oven for 5 minutes. Remove the baking sheet from oven, and carefully add the Brussels sprouts to the hot baking sheet with bacon. Sprinkle with the garlic, salt, and pepper, and carefully toss the bacon and Brussels sprouts until coated in bacon fat. (Be careful not to touch the hot pan while doing this.) Return the baking sheet to the oven, and roast for 15 minutes.

3. Meanwhile, in a small bowl, combine the vinegar and honey. Remove the baking sheet from the oven, drizzle the vinegar mixture over the Brussels sprouts, and carefully toss. Return the baking sheet to the oven for 5 minutes more. Brussels sprouts are done when they are tender, and the edges turn brown.

NOTE
To store, refrigerate in an airtight container for up to 1 week.

VARIATION
Toss the warm Brussels sprouts with goat cheese or blue cheese crumbles for a flavor explosion you won't believe! For even more bacon flavor, toss them with Warm Bacon Dressing (page 123).

Meaty Mushrooms

When cooked properly, umami-rich mushrooms can develop a flavor and texture that is reminiscent of meat. Worcestershire sauce and garlic bring out the meaty flavor of mushrooms in this recipe, and roasting them makes preparation simple and foolproof. Make these mushrooms a part of your weekly meal prep to toss in salads or garnish soups.

Prep time **15 minutes** • Cook time **30 minutes** • Yield **2 cups** • Serving size **½ cup**

- 1lb (450g) white mushrooms, sliced
- 1lb (450g) cremini mushrooms, sliced
- 1½ tsp extra-virgin olive oil
- 1 tbsp Worcestershire sauce
- 3 cloves garlic, minced
- 1 tsp kosher salt
- ½ tsp freshly ground black pepper
- 4 sprigs fresh thyme

1. Preheat the oven to 400°F (200°C). Line 2 baking sheets with foil.

2. In a large bowl, toss the mushrooms with the olive oil, Worcestershire sauce, garlic, salt, pepper, and thyme. Spread the mushrooms on the prepared baking sheets in a single layer. Roast for 25 to 30 minutes. The mushrooms will shrink and brown.

3. Remove the mushrooms from the oven, and carefully remove the thyme stems. Transfer the mushrooms to a bowl, and serve warm or at room temperature.

NOTES
You can use any medley of mushrooms for this recipe. I especially enjoy using hen-of-the-woods, shiitake, and morel mushrooms.

Meaty Mushrooms go well with Cast Iron–Seared Steak (page 78) or Roasted Chicken with Root Veggies (page 69). They are also terrific stuffed in Loaded Potato Skins (page 27) or as a garnish on top of Herby Risotto (page 68).

Leftover mushrooms can be refrigerated in an airtight container for up to 1 week.

Roasted Garlic Grits

Ever make something for someone else and feel sad 'cause you don't have any for yourself? That's how I felt when I made these for a client's dinner party. They were so good! I was sad that I didn't have any and mad at myself for not thinking of this recipe sooner. I have not forgotten it since, and I am so glad that you have it now. Just serve this with everything. You don't need anything else, just these grits. That's all.

Prep time **15 minutes** • Cook time **50 minutes** • Yield **6 cups** • Serving size **1 cup**

1 bulb garlic

1 tsp extra-virgin olive oil

1 tbsp + 1 tsp kosher salt

3 cups chicken stock (for **Homemade Chicken Stock,** see page 124)

⊕ 1½ cups whole milk

½ cup butter

⊕ 1½ cups old-fashioned grits

⊕ ½ cup heavy cream

½ cup grated Parmesan cheese

1. Preheat the oven to 400°F (200°C).

2. Cut the garlic bulb in half horizontally, creating a top and bottom half. Place the bottom half of the garlic bulb on a small piece of aluminum foil. Drizzle with olive oil and sprinkle with 1 teaspoon salt. Place the top half of the garlic bulb on the seasoned bottom half, and wrap the entire bulb tightly with foil. Place the foil-wrapped garlic in the oven and roast for 25 to 30 minutes. The garlic should be very soft, tender, and squeezable. Remove from the oven and allow to cool.

3. In a medium saucepan, heat the chicken stock, milk, butter, and remaining 1 tablespoon salt over medium-high heat. Allow the liquid to come to a boil, being careful not to overboil. When boiling, quickly whisk in the grits and reduce the heat to low. Simmer for 20 to 25 minutes, stirring occasionally, until thick.

4. Squeeze the roasted garlic into the cooked grits. (The garlic should easily squeeze out of its papery peel.) Add the cream and Parmesan cheese, and stir well to combine. Serve hot.

NOTE
To store, refrigerate in an airtight container for up to 1 week. Stir in 2 to 3 tablespoons stock or milk when reheating.

VARIATION
To make fried grit cakes, spread leftover grits on a baking sheet and smooth with an offset spatula. Refrigerate for 4 hours. Use a biscuit cutter or drinking glass to cut the grits into rounds. Sear the grit cakes on each side in a skillet over medium-low heat with bacon fat or butter.

Potatoes au Gratin

I prefer au gratin potatoes over mashed potatoes. I know...shocker! Let's unpack this. Mashed potatoes are fantastic and have their own time and place. They include two of my favorite ingredients: cream and butter. But potatoes au gratin have the wonderful addition of cheese. Two kinds of cheese give these irresistible potatoes a beautiful crispy crust and an added layer of flavor.

Prep time **30 minutes** • Cook time **40 minutes** • Yield **1 9 × 13-in (23 × 33cm) casserole** • Serving size **½ cup**

⊕ 1½ cups heavy cream

⊕ 2 sprigs fresh thyme

2 whole cloves garlic

⊕ ¼ tsp freshly grated nutmeg

1 tbsp butter

4 tbsp shredded Parmesan cheese, divided

⊕ 1½ cups shredded cheddar cheese, divided

2lb (1k) Yukon Gold potatoes, sliced ⅛in (3mm) thick

3 tsp kosher salt, divided

1½ tsp freshly grated black pepper, divided

1. Preheat the oven to 400°F (200°C) degrees. To a small saucepan, add the cream, thyme, garlic, and nutmeg. Bring to a low simmer over medium heat.

2. While the cream mixture is simmering, grease a 9 × 13-inch (23 × 33cm) baking dish with the butter. Sprinkle 1 tablespoon Parmesan cheese in the bottom of the baking dish. In a small bowl, mix the remaining 3 tablespoons Parmesan with ¾ cup cheddar.

3. Cover the bottom of the dish with a single layer of potato slices, and season with 1 teaspoon salt and ½ teaspoon pepper. Sprinkle approximately ¼ cup of the cheese mixture on top of the potatoes.

4. Remove the thyme stems and garlic cloves from the simmering cream. Pour about one-third of the cream mixture over the potatoes. Repeat the layers of potatoes, salt and pepper, cheese, and cream until the casserole dish is full. (This usually takes 3 layers.) Finish the top layer with the remaining cheese mixture.

5. Cover the dish with foil and bake for 30 minutes. Remove the dish from the oven and remove the foil. Sprinkle the remaining ¾ cup cheddar cheese over the top of the bubbling potatoes, and bake uncovered for 10 minutes more.

NOTES

Add more cheese! Trust me on this. You can add up to 1 cup of additional shredded cheese. Try another variety, such as Gouda, Gruyère, or Swiss.

To store, wrap the dish tightly with foil or transfer to an airtight container, and refrigerate for up to 1 week.

VARIATION

This recipe is also delicious when made with sweet potatoes. If using sweet potatoes, replace the cheddar with Gouda or Gruyère.

Broccoli Rice Casserole

Step aside, "cream of whatever" soup. This casserole features a scratch-made cheese sauce that is quick to prepare and delivers the homey and comforting casserole vibe that your family and guests will love and appreciate. The buttery cracker-crumb topping provides a lovely texture to this creamy dish.

Prep time **20 minutes** • Cook time **1 hour** • Yield **1 9 × 13-in (23 × 33cm) casserole** • Serving size **1 cup**

3 tbsp butter, plus more to grease the dish

⊕ 4 cups fresh or frozen broccoli florets

1 small yellow onion, diced

2 cloves garlic, minced

3 tbsp all-purpose flour

2 tsp granulated garlic

½ tsp onion powder

½ tsp paprika

2½ tsp kosher salt

½ tsp freshly ground black pepper

⊕ 2 cups whole milk

1 tbsp Worcestershire sauce

2 tsp Dijon mustard

⊕ 4oz (110g) cream cheese

⊕ 2 cups shredded sharp cheddar cheese, divided

3 cups cooked rice (any variety)

For the topping

4 tbsp butter

⊕ 1 cup crushed Ritz crackers or other butter cracker

½ cup grated Parmesan cheese

1. Preheat the oven to 350°F (175°C). Grease a 9 × 13-inch (23 × 33cm) baking dish with butter.

2. If using fresh broccoli, blanch the broccoli in a large pot of boiling water. Leave the broccoli in the pot for 30 to 45 seconds, and then use a slotted spoon to transfer it to a large bowl filled with water and ice. Drain the broccoli using a colander and set aside.

3. In a medium saucepan, melt the butter over medium heat. Add the onion and minced garlic, and cook for 1 to 2 minutes or until the onion starts to become tender and translucent. Sprinkle the flour over the onion and garlic and whisk it into the butter. Cook for 1 minute more. Whisk in the granulated garlic, onion powder, paprika, salt, and pepper. Slowly add the milk, and increase the heat to medium-high. The milk should begin to thicken and form a sauce. Reduce the heat to low. Stir in the Worcestershire sauce, mustard, cream cheese, and 1 cup cheddar cheese. Remove the cheese sauce from the heat.

4. Stir in the broccoli and rice until everything is thoroughly combined. Transfer the mixture to the prepared baking dish, and sprinkle with the remaining 1 cup cheddar cheese.

5. To make the topping, in a small bowl, microwave the butter until melted. Stir in the crushed crackers and Parmesan cheese. Sprinkle the buttered crumbs over the casserole. Bake for 30 minutes or until golden brown and bubbly.

NOTES

To store, refrigerate in an airtight container for up to 1 week.

To freeze, prepare the casserole in a freezer-safe baking dish. Cool to room temperature, and then wrap tightly with plastic wrap and aluminum foil. Freeze for up to 3 months. Thaw in the refrigerator 1 day before baking.

Three-Cheese Soufflé

Light, fluffy, and decadent, a well-executed soufflé is the perfect example of how a few simple ingredients can produce a truly impressive dish. Although soufflés require technique, patience, and effort, the result is worth it. In this three-cheese soufflé, pungent Gruyère, robust Parmesan, and sharp cheddar come together to make a pillow of cheesy goodness. My advice: be fearless. Be patient. You've got this.

Prep time **30 minutes** • Cook time **25 minutes** • Yield **6 8oz (235ml) soufflés** • Serving size **1 soufflé**

5 tbsp butter, divided

½ cup finely grated Parmesan cheese, divided

⊕ 2 cups whole milk

2 tbsp all-purpose flour

⊕ ½ cup grated Gruyère cheese

⊕ ½ cup grated cheddar cheese

½ tsp kosher salt

1 tsp Worcestershire sauce

⊕ 5 eggs, whites and yolks separated

⊕ ½ tsp cream of tartar

1. Remove the top and center rack from the oven, leaving only the bottom rack. Preheat the oven to 350°F (175°C). Use 1 tablespoon butter to grease six 8-ounce (235ml) ramekins. (You can substitute a 1½-qt soufflé dish.) Dust all sides of the ramekins with ¼ cup Parmesan cheese and shake off any excess.

2. In a medium saucepan, heat the milk over low heat until warm.

3. In a large saucepan, melt the remaining 4 tablespoons butter over medium-low heat. Add the flour, and whisk until it forms a paste. Continue cooking for 1 minute more. Slowly whisk in the warm milk until all of the paste has dissolved. Increase the heat to medium, and bring to a simmer. It will thicken slightly. Whisk in the Gruyère cheese, cheddar cheese, and remaining ¼ cup Parmesan cheese. Whisk until melted. Whisk in the salt and Worcestershire sauce. Remove the pan from the heat and allow it to cool slightly, about 5 minutes.

4. While the mixture is cooling, in the clean bowl of a stand mixer, whip the egg whites and cream of tartar for 4 to 5 minutes until stiff peaks form.

5. One at a time, whisk the egg yolks into the slightly cooled sauce mixture. Fold one-fourth of the whipped egg whites into the sauce mixture, taking care not to lose the egg white peaks. Repeat until all of the egg whites have been incorporated.

6. Transfer the batter to the prepared ramekins, and place the ramekins on a baking sheet. Bake for 25 minutes until the soufflés are puffed and golden brown. Do not open the oven door for the first 20 minutes of baking; instead, use the oven light to gauge the doneness of the soufflés. They are done when they are golden brown on top and the centers jiggle slightly when shaken. Serve immediately.

Condiments & Fixin's

Apple Cider Vinaigrette

I created this vinaigrette for the Autumn Butter Lettuce Salad (page 94), but it's terrific with any blend of greens and veggies, and it also works as a marinade. There is a very slight sweetness from the honey and a punch of flavor from the apple cider vinegar and Dijon mustard.

Prep time **10 minutes** • Cook time **none** • Yield **1½ cups** • Serving size **2 tbsp**

½ cup apple cider vinegar

1 tbsp Dijon mustard

2 tbsp honey

2 cloves garlic

⊕ 1 cup grapeseed or avocado oil

1 tsp kosher salt

½ tsp freshly ground black pepper

1. In a blender, combine the vinegar, mustard, honey, and garlic. Blend until the garlic is minced and the mixture is well blended. Remove the pour cap from the blender and slowly drizzle in the oil. Continue blending until the dressing thickens slightly.

2. Turn off the blender and pour the vinaigrette into a small bowl for serving or a glass jar for storage. Stir in the salt and pepper.

NOTE
Refrigerate in an airtight container for up to 2 weeks.

VARIATION
This dressing is also excellent made with olive oil and/or another type of vinegar. Try white wine vinegar, red wine vinegar, balsamic vinegar, or golden balsamic vinegar for a different but still delicious flavor profile.

Warm Bacon Dressing

If you ever have a dinner party and have a nonsalad eater at your table, plan to make this dressing. That picky eater will ask to take leftover salad home. This dressing is delicious on many salads, especially those made with dark leafy greens, like spinach or collards. It's also pretty tasty spooned over Maple Bourbon Mashed Sweet Potatoes (page 106) or Bacon Balsamic Brussels Sprouts (page 112).

Prep time **10 minutes** • Cook time **15 minutes** • Yield **¾ cup** • Serving size **1 tbsp**

4 strips thick-cut bacon or 6 strips regular bacon, chopped

3 cloves garlic, finely minced

1 tbsp honey

2 tbsp brown sugar

2 tbsp Dijon mustard

¼ cup apple cider vinegar

1 tsp Worcestershire sauce

1 tsp kosher salt

½ tsp freshly ground black pepper

1. Place a medium saucepan over medium heat. Add the bacon and cook for 12 minutes until the fat has rendered and each piece is crispy. Using a slotted spoon, transfer the bacon to a paper towel–lined plate to drain.

2. Return the pan to the heat and quickly add the garlic, honey, brown sugar, mustard, vinegar, Worcestershire, salt, and pepper while whisking vigorously. Cook for 1 minute or until the dressing thickens, and then remove from the heat. Add the bacon to the pan and stir. Transfer the dressing to a heat-safe container for serving or storage.

NOTE
Refrigerate in an airtight container for up to 5 days. Heat refrigerated dressing in the microwave for 30 seconds before use.

Homemade Chicken Stock

Good chicken stock is the basis of so many recipes. It is used for soups and sauces, to cook grains, and so much more. Making your own chicken stock is a great way to use every bit of the ingredients you purchase, whether you have store-bought rotisserie chicken or you've made Roast Chicken with Root Veggies (page 69). Double this recipe and keep a few quarts in the freezer.

Prep time **20 minutes** • Cook time **6 hours** • Yield **2 quarts (2l)** • Serving size **1 cup**

⊕ 1 chicken carcass

1 tsp extra-virgin olive oil

⊕ 3 large carrots, unpeeled, cut into large pieces

1 large onion, cut into large pieces

2 bulbs garlic, cut in half

⊕ 5 celery stalks with leaves

⊕ 1 bunch of fresh parsley

⊕ 5 sprigs fresh thyme

2 bay leaves

2 tbsp kosher salt

1 tsp whole black peppercorns

1. Preheat the oven to 400°F (200°C). Line a baking sheet with foil.

2. Place the chicken carcass and any remaining pieces of chicken on the prepared baking sheet and drizzle with olive oil. Rub the oil over the chicken bones and pieces. Roast for 20 minutes.

3. Place the roasted chicken carcass and pieces into a large stockpot. Add the carrots, onion, garlic, celery, parsley, thyme, bay leaves, salt, and peppercorns to the pot. Add water to cover all the ingredients by at least 1 inch (2.5cm).

4. Bring the water to a boil. Once the water is boiling, reduce the heat to low. Simmer, uncovered, for at least 6 hours.

5. Using a fine mesh strainer, strain the stock into a large bowl or pot. (Discard the solids.) Allow the liquid to cool completely before transferring to freezer-safe containers for storage. If freezing, do not fill the containers to the brim to ensure room for the stock to expand as it freezes.

NOTES

Add a couple of cleaned leeks if you have them on hand.

I like to start stock early in the day and let it cook until I am ready for bed. I turn it off a few hours before I'm ready to sleep to allow it time to cool before storing it in the fridge. I strain it and set it up for the freezer the next day.

To store, refrigerate in an airtight container for up to 2 weeks. Freeze for up to 6 months.

VARIATION

The same method can be used to make beef stock using beef bones or shrimp stock using shrimp shells.

Homemade Mayo

It's easy to make mayonnaise. You don't need many ingredients, there isn't any cooking involved, and it tastes richer and more flavorful than anything you can buy at the store.

Prep time **10 minutes** • Cook time **none** • Yield **1 cup** • Serving size **1 tbsp**

⊕ 1 egg

2 tbsp white vinegar or the juice of 1 lemon

1 cup canola oil

⊕ 1 tsp mustard powder

1 tsp granulated garlic

1½ tsp kosher salt

½ tsp freshly ground black pepper

In a food processor or high-speed blender, combine the egg and vinegar. Blend on high for 1 to 2 minutes or until the mixture turns light yellow. Reduce the speed to low. Remove the pour cap, and slowly drizzle in the oil. Continue blending for 15 to 20 seconds. The mixture should begin to thicken, and the sound of the motor will change. Add the mustard powder, garlic, salt, and pepper. Blend until all of the seasonings are evenly distributed.

NOTE

To store, refrigerate an airtight container for up to 2 weeks.

Parmesan Ranch Dressing

My Parmesan ranch dressing is thick, creamy, slightly tangy, and works beautifully as the universal condiment of the Midwest.

Prep time **20 minutes** • Cook time **none** • Yield **1½ cups** • Serving size **2 tbsp**

⊕ 1 cup mayonnaise (for **Homemade Mayo**, see above)

⊕ ½ cup sour cream

1 clove garlic

⊕ ¼ cup minced fresh dill

⊕ ¼ cup minced fresh flat-leaf parsley

⊕ Juice of 1 lemon

2 tsp red wine vinegar

½ tsp granulated garlic

¼ tsp onion powder

½ tsp kosher salt

¼ tsp freshly ground black pepper

1 cup grated Parmesan cheese

In a food processor, combine the mayonnaise, sour cream, garlic clove, dill, and parsley. Process for 1 minute. Add the lemon juice, vinegar, granulated garlic, onion powder, salt, and pepper. Process ingredients just until combined. Transfer the dressing to a bowl and stir in the Parmesan cheese.

NOTES

Serve with Crispy Oven-Baked Chicken Wings (page 33), Fresh-Cut Fries (page 98), or Fried Okra (page 109).

This dressing can be chilled or eaten right away. To store, refrigerate in an airtight container for up to 2 weeks.

VARIATION

For a tangy buttermilk ranch dressing, omit the Parmesan cheese and red wine vinegar, and add ½ cup buttermilk.

Roasted Garlic Aioli

Roasted garlic makes this aioli extra special. It lends a slight sweetness, which is a perfect contrast to the zingy tartness of the lemon.

Prep time **15 minutes** • Cook time **30 minutes** • Yield **1 cup** • Serving size **1 tbsp**

1 large bulb garlic

½ tsp extra-virgin olive oil

2 tsp kosher salt, divided

⊕ 1 egg

⊕ 1 tbsp lemon juice

⊕ ½ cup grapeseed or avocado oil

½ tsp freshly ground black pepper

1 tsp granulated garlic

1. Preheat the oven to 400°F (200°C). Cut garlic bulb in half horizontally. Drizzle the cut sides with olive oil, and sprinkle with 1 teaspoon salt. Bring the garlic bulb together and wrap with foil. Roast for 25 to 30 minutes until tender and lightly browned.

2. In a blender or food processor, blend the egg and lemon juice for 1 to 2 minutes until the mixture turns light yellow. Reduce the speed to low, and slowly drizzle in the grapeseed oil. Continue blending for 20 to 30 seconds. The mixture should begin to thicken, and the sound of the blender will change. Season with the remaining 1 teaspoon salt, pepper, and granulated garlic. Squeeze the roasted garlic into the mixture, and blend until just incorporated.

NOTE
To store, refrigerate in an airtight container for up to 2 weeks.

Homemade Tartar Sauce

Basic pantry ingredients are all it takes to create a zesty tartar sauce that's delicious with fried fish, roasted fish, hushpuppies, and even French fries.

Prep time **10 minutes** • Cook time **none** • Yield **1 cup** • Serving size **1 tbsp**

⊕ 1 cup mayonnaise (for **Homemade Mayo,** see page 126)

2 tsp Dijon mustard

⊕ Juice of ½ lemon

⊕ ¼ cup dill pickle relish

⊕ 2 tbsp capers, chopped + 1 tsp caper juice

1 tsp salt

½ tsp freshly ground black pepper

1 tsp granulated garlic

⊕ 1 tbsp minced fresh dill

To a small bowl, add all ingredients and stir until thoroughly combined. Cover with plastic wrap and refrigerate for 30 minutes before serving.

NOTE
To store, refrigerate in an airtight container for up to 2 weeks.

Refrigerator Pickles

Pickles are very easy to make, especially if you already have the staple ingredients on hand. This recipe calls for cucumbers, but almost any veggie can be pickled.

Prep time **15 minutes** • Cook time **5 minutes** • Yield **1 quart (1l)** • Serving size **¼ cup**

½ cup white vinegar
½ cup apple cider vinegar
1 cup water
1 tbsp kosher salt
½ tsp whole black peppercorns
⊕ ¼ tsp red pepper flakes (more if you like a little heat)
¼ cup granulated sugar
4 large cloves garlic
2 bay leaves
⊕ 6–8 pickling cucumbers, cut into rounds or spears

1. In a medium pot, combine all ingredients except for the cucumbers. Bring the liquid to a boil. When boiling, remove from the heat and cool for 10 to 15 minutes.

2. Place the cucumbers in a clean quart-size Mason jar or deli container. Pour the cooled pickling liquid over the cucumbers and secure the lid. The cucumbers should be fully submerged in the pickling liquid. Pickles can be eaten after marinating for 1 hour, but are best after being refrigerated for 7 days. Keep refrigerated for up to 3 weeks.

Pickled Red Onions

These quick-pickled onions are an excellent garnish or condiment on so many different things. I often use them in place of pickles.

Prep time **10 minutes** • Cook time **5 minutes** • Yield **1 cup** • Serving size **1 tbsp**

1 cup red wine vinegar
1 cup water
1 clove garlic
1 tbsp granulated sugar
1 tsp kosher salt
1 bay leaf
1 large red onion, sliced thinly

1. To a small saucepan, add the vinegar, water, garlic, sugar, and salt. Heat over medium-high heat, stirring until the sugar and salt are dissolved. Bring the liquid to a boil, and then remove from the heat. Cool for 10 minutes.

2. Place the onion in a medium heat-safe bowl. Add the pickling liquid, making sure that the onion is fully submerged. Marinate for at least 20 minutes up to 1 hour. Refrigerate in an airtight container for up to 2 weeks. (I prefer to discard the pickling liquid before storage.)

Balsamic Reduction

You can buy premade balsamic reduction, but why would you when you have balsamic vinegar and brown sugar as pantry staples? These two ingredients come together to create a deeply flavorful condiment that complements everything from roasted vegetables to grilled meats. This should sit right next to Pickled Red Onions (page 129) as an everyday condiment in your refrigerator.

Prep time **5 minutes** • Cook time **8–10 minutes** • Yield **½ cup** • Serving size **2 tsp**

1 cup balsamic vinegar
2 tbsp brown sugar
¼ tsp kosher salt

In a small saucepan, combine all ingredients and place over medium-high heat, stirring until the sugar is dissolved. Allow the mixture to come to a boil, and cook for 4 to 5 minutes more. The liquid should reduce by about half. Remove from the heat and transfer to a heat-safe container. The vinegar reduction will thicken as it cools.

NOTES
To store, refrigerate in an airtight container for up to 3 weeks.

Drizzle this reduction on Herby Risotto (page 68), Smoky Sweet Potato Soup (page 57), Maple Bourbon Mashed Sweet Potatoes (page 106), or Meaty Mushrooms (page 114).

Caramelized Onions

Did you know that onions could be buttery? Butter is what I think of when I make these, and it makes me want to put them on everything. Try caramelized onions on grilled cheese, burgers, and crostini for luxurious texture and deep, sweet, oniony flavor.

Prep time **15 minutes** • Cook time **30 minutes** • Yield **1 cup** • Serving size **1 tbsp**

1 tsp extra-virgin olive oil
3 large sweet onions, thinly sliced
2 cloves garlic, minced
1 tsp kosher salt
½ tsp freshly ground black pepper
Balsamic vinegar (optional), to finish

In a medium skillet, heat the olive oil over medium-low heat. Add the onion and garlic, and toss until coated in oil. Cook for 30 to 40 minutes, stirring occasionally, until the onions are browned and tender. Season with salt, pepper, and a splash of balsamic vinegar, if using.

NOTE
I prefer sweet onions, but this method will work with any type of onion. You can also use shallots.

To store, refrigerate in an airtight container for up to 1 week.

Sweet Onion Ketchup

I've been trying to make ketchup fancy since I was a kid. When we had fries at home, I would take granulated garlic and add it to store-bought ketchup. I thought I was super gourmet! Now that I love making sauces, I'm proud to make real gourmet ketchup. This sweet onion version has a bit of texture and a balanced sweetness that you don't find in the store-bought variety.

Prep time **5 minutes** • Cook time **25–30 minutes** • Yield **1 cup** • Serving size **1 tbsp**

1 tsp extra-virgin olive oil

¼ cup diced yellow onion

1 (6oz; 170g) can tomato paste

1½ cups water (you can just fill up the tomato paste can twice to get all the good stuff out)

⅓ cup apple cider vinegar

2 tbsp balsamic vinegar

¼ cup brown sugar

3 tbsp honey

1 tbsp onion powder

1 tbsp granulated garlic

2 tsp smoked paprika

1. To a small saucepan, add the olive oil then the onion and cook over medium heat for 3 to 5 minutes until tender and slightly translucent. Add the tomato paste and water, and whisk together until combined. Add the apple cider vinegar, balsamic vinegar, brown sugar, honey, onion powder, granulated garlic, and paprika. Increase the heat, and bring to a boil. When boiling, reduce the heat to medium-low, and cook until the mixture has reduced by about half, about 20 minutes.

2. Remove from the heat and allow to cool slightly. Using an immersion blender, blend the mixture until smooth. (If you do not have an immersion blender, use a regular blender. Remove the cap, and cover the hole in the lid with a dish towel to allow steam to escape.)

NOTES

Add ½ teaspoon cayenne if you want a little kick to your ketchup.

Serve with Fresh-Cut Fries (page 98) or on The Juiciest Turkey Burger You've Ever Had (page 53).

To store, refrigerate in an airtight container for up to 1 month.

BBQ Sauce

There are several ways to make BBQ sauce, and I enjoy playing around with all of them. This recipe stands up on its own, but it can also be an excellent base for all sorts of BBQ sauce experimenting you plan to do.

Prep time **10 minutes** • Cook time **25 minutes—2 hours** • Yield **2½ cups** • Serving size **2 tbsp**

2 tsp extra-virgin olive oil

1 yellow onion, chopped

4 cloves garlic, minced

⊕ 3 tbsp **Savory Dry Rub** (page 135)

2 tbsp Worcestershire sauce

1 tsp soy sauce

3 tbsp apple cider vinegar

1 tbsp balsamic vinegar

⊕ 1 tbsp yellow mustard

2 tbsp honey

⊕ 2 cups ketchup

¼ cup water

1½ cups brown sugar

1. In a medium saucepan, heat the olive oil over medium heat. When hot, add the onion and sauté for 5 minutes or until they start to become translucent. Add the garlic and cook for 1 minute. Add the dry rub, Worcestershire sauce, soy sauce, vinegars, and mustard. Cook for 30 to 45 seconds. Stir in the honey, ketchup, and water, and reduce the heat to low. Simmer for 10 minutes, stirring occasionally.

2. Stir in the brown sugar, and continue to cook over low heat for at least 15 minutes or up to 2 hours, stirring occasionally. The sauce will continue to develop flavor as it cooks. Transfer to a lidded glass jar for storage.

NOTES

If you have bacon fat on hand, it can be used in place of the olive oil.

This sauce has a bit of texture from the onion and garlic. If you like a completely smooth BBQ sauce, use an immersion blender to purée the sauce to your preferred consistency.

To store, refrigerate in an airtight container for up to 2 weeks.

Bacon Jam

This belongs on everything. It really does. Bacon jam is basically bacon-y goodness cooked down to become a gooey, savory, salty-sweet condiment. It can be served on biscuits, toast, pancakes, waffles, grilled cheese, and burgers, or included in a charcuterie spread.

Prep time **30 minutes** • Cook time **1 hour 30 minutes** • Yield **3–4 cups** • Serving size **1 tbsp**

1 lb (450g) bacon, chopped

3 onions, chopped

2 cloves garlic, minced

¼ cup balsamic vinegar

½ cup water

½ cup brown sugar

⊕ ¼ cup maple syrup

⊕ ½ tsp stone-ground mustard

1. Heat a large skillet over medium-high heat. Add the bacon, and cook for 10 to 12 minutes until the fat has rendered and the bacon is fully cooked. Transfer to a paper towel–lined plate to drain, leaving 1 tablespoon rendered fat in the pan. Add the onion and garlic, and cook for 2 to 3 minutes or until the onion is tender and translucent.

2. Add the vinegar to the pan, and scrape up all of the yummy bacon and onion bits from the bottom. Stir in the water, brown sugar, and maple syrup. When the mixture begins to bubble, add the mustard and reserved cooked bacon pieces. Reduce the heat to low, and cook for about 60 minutes, stirring occasionally, until the mixture reaches a jam-like consistency. (It will continue to thicken as it cools.)

NOTES

You can use honey instead of maple syrup in this recipe. Do not substitute granulated sugar for brown sugar.

To store, refrigerate in an airtight container for up to 2 weeks.

Taco Seasoning

Packets of premixed taco seasoning can be found in millions of household pantries. Many people consider them a staple ingredient. The problem is that those little packets contain additives as well as herbs and spices. This gluten-free blend is perfect for seasoning ground meat to make tacos, but it can also be used to add a bold flavor to chili, pulled chicken, or grilled shrimp.

Prep time **10 minutes** • Cook time **none** • Yield **⅓ cup** • Serving size **2 tbsp**

- 2 tbsp chili powder
- 1 tbsp granulated garlic
- 2½ tsp ground cumin
- 2 tsp smoked paprika
- 2 tsp onion powder
- 1 tsp dried oregano
- ½ tsp ground coriander
- ½ tsp freshly ground black pepper
- ¼ tsp cayenne (optional)

In a small bowl, combine all ingredients and stir until evenly blended. Transfer to an airtight container for storage.

NOTES
The seasoning blend can be stored in a cool, dry place for up to 3 months.

Use 2 tablespoons per 1 pound (450g) ground meat for tacos.

Savory Dry Rub

This savory dry rub is a staple in my spice cabinet. I use it as an all-purpose seasoning as well as a BBQ dry rub. It works so well on chicken, pork, and beef. It's even delicious sprinkled on roasted potatoes.

Prep time **10 minutes** • Cook time **none** • Yield **1¼ cups** • Serving size **1 tbsp**

- ½ cup granulated garlic
- ¼ cup smoked paprika
- 2 tbsp chili powder
- 2 tbsp onion powder
- 1 tbsp mustard powder
- 1 tbsp ground cumin
- 1 tbsp vinegar powder (see note)
- ¼ cup kosher salt
- 1 tbsp freshly ground black pepper

Combine all ingredients in an airtight container and stir until spices are evenly blended. Store in a cool, dry place for up to 6 months.

NOTE
Vinegar powder can be purchased online. It's worth having in my spice cabinet, but I don't use it as often as staple spices.

VARIATION
Add ½ cup brown sugar for a little sweetness, especially when using this rub for BBQ.

Vanilla Extract

This recipe doesn't make use of any staple ingredients, but it only requires two ingredients to make, and it is a pantry staple in its own right. There is nothing like the aroma of homemade vanilla extract. I love opening my airtight bottle and smelling the combination of bourbon and vanilla. It packs a punch every time I use it.

Prep time **10 minutes** + **2–6 months** • Cook time **none** • Yield **8fl oz (240ml)** • Serving size **1 tsp**

- 5 whole vanilla bean pods
- 8fl oz (240ml) bourbon

1. Split each vanilla bean pod down the middle, lengthwise, leaving them intact. There should only be a slight split in each pod to expose the seeds. Trim the ends of the pods if needed to fit them into your airtight bottle or jar.

2. Add all five pods to an airtight glass bottle or jar. (A narrow bottle with a swing-top lid is ideal.) Using a funnel, add the bourbon, making sure the pods are fully submerged.

3. Store at room temperature in a cool, dry place away from direct sunlight. The vanilla will be ready to use after 2 months, but let the pods soak for 6 months for the best possible flavor. Use as directed in any recipe that calls for vanilla extract.

NOTE
Vanilla bean pods can be reused a few times; just refill the bottle with bourbon. When the pods begin to feel and look slimy, remove them from the bottle and discard them.

VARIATION
Vodka, brandy, or rum can be used in place of bourbon. Choose a spirit that suits your taste.

Desserts

Chocolate Lava Cakes

These impressive little cakes used to intimidate me. Then I finally made them. I cannot tell you how easy they are to make. They are a go-to for my client dinner parties because I can make them ahead, and there is always a fun presentation factor. I promise that you will have these mastered in no time.

Prep time **20 minutes** • Cook time **8–12 minutes** • Yield **6 cakes** • Serving size **1 cake**

5 tbsp butter, softened, divided

⅓ cup + 1 tbsp granulated sugar, divided

⊕ 3 large eggs, at room temperature

⊕ 8oz (225g) semi-sweet chocolate

⅓ cup all-purpose flour

¼ tsp salt

⊕ 1 tsp instant coffee dissolved in 2 tsp water

1 tbsp pure vanilla extract (for **Vanilla Extract**, see page 137)

⊕ Powdered sugar (optional), for dusting

1. Preheat the oven to 400°F (200°C). Generously butter six 4-ounce (120ml) ramekins using 1 tablespoon butter. Sprinkle with 1 tablespoon granulated sugar and tap out the excess. Set aside.

2. In the bowl of a stand mixer, cream together the remaining 4 tablespoons butter and remaining ⅓ cup granulated sugar until light and fluffy. Turn off the mixer and scrape down the sides of the bowl to ensure the butter and sugar are fully incorporated. Add the eggs one at a time, making sure the whole egg is incorporated before adding the next. Scrape down the sides of the bowl between each egg.

3. Place the chocolate in a microwave-safe bowl. Heat the chocolate in the microwave in 30-second intervals, stirring between each interval, until the chocolate has fully melted.

4. With the mixer on low speed, add the flour and salt and mix until just combined. Fold in the melted chocolate. Be sure to scrape down the sides of the bowl. Mix in the coffee and vanilla.

5. Divide the batter evenly among the prepared ramekins. Place the ramekins on a baking sheet, and put the baking sheet in the oven. Bake for 8 to 12 minutes. After 8 minutes, check the cakes every 60 seconds. The cakes are done when the tops are set and the centers are just slightly jiggly. Take care not to overbake.

6. Let the cakes cool for 15 to 20 minutes before inverting onto a plate, or serve them directly from the ramekins. Dust with powdered sugar before serving.

NOTE
To make ahead, fill each ramekin with batter, and place them on a baking sheet. Cover with plastic wrap and refrigerate for up to 12 hours. Remove from the refrigerator 1 hour before baking.

VARIATION
In place of instant coffee, consider using 2 teaspoons of a liquor such as Irish cream, Grand Marnier, or Kahlua.

Sour Cream Banana Bread

My dad and I have a thing for banana bread. The bread must have nuts, and there must be softened butter to slather on a warm slice. This recipe guarantees perfectly moist and crumbly bread every single time. Extra-ripe bananas ensure that the banana flavor truly shines. While walnuts are traditional in banana-nut bread, Dad and I go for pecans.

Prep time **20 minutes** • Cook time **1 hour 15 minutes** • Yield **1 9-inch (23cm) loaf** • Serving size **1 slice**

¾ cup butter, softened, plus more to grease the pan

2 cups all-purpose flour, plus more for dusting

1½ tsp baking powder

½ tsp kosher salt

1 tsp ground cinnamon

⊕ ½ tsp ground nutmeg

⊕ 4 large extra-ripe bananas

½ cup granulated sugar

½ cup brown sugar

⊕ ½ cup sour cream

⊕ 2 large eggs, at room temperature

⊕ 1 tsp vanilla extract (for **Vanilla Extract,** see page 137)

⊕ ½ cup pecans, toasted and chopped (optional)

1. Preheat the oven to 350°F (175°C). Prepare a loaf pan by greasing it with butter and dusting it with flour. Shake off any excess flour.

2. In a large bowl, whisk together the flour, baking powder, salt, cinnamon, and nutmeg. Set aside.

3. Place the bananas in the bowl of a stand mixer. Use the paddle attachment to mash them at low speed. Add the butter, granulated sugar, and brown sugar, and cream together at medium-low speed. Increase the speed to medium, and continue mixing until the bananas and sugars are well blended. This will take 2 to 3 minutes. Add the sour cream, and continue mixing. Beat in the eggs one at a time until fully incorporated. Add the vanilla, and stir for an additional 30 seconds.

4. Add the flour mixture to the banana mixture ½ cup at a time, and mix at low speed. Repeat until all of the flour has been mixed in. Turn off the mixer as soon as streaks of flour are no longer visible. Take care not to overmix the batter. Fold in the pecans, if using.

5. Pour the batter into the prepared loaf pan and bake for 60 to 75 minutes. The bread is done when a toothpick inserted in the center of the loaf comes out clean. Let the bread cool in the pan for 10 to 15 minutes before transferring it to a wire rack to finish cooling. (Bread can be sliced while still warm, but do not slice it when hot.)

NOTES
Reheat the bread, by the slice, in the microwave for 20 seconds or in the toaster oven on medium heat for 1 to 2 minutes.

Wrap tightly with plastic wrap, then aluminum foil, and store in a cool, dry place for up to 1 week.

VARIATION
Fold in ½ cup dried cranberries for a little extra zing.

Zucchini Bread

I love banana bread, but zucchini reigns supreme for me. I think I was the only kid who didn't freak out when my mom told me there was a vegetable in the bread I was eating for breakfast. Zucchini bread makes a great breakfast because the warm spices perfectly complement a cup of coffee or glass of milk. The zucchini takes on the sweetness from the brown sugar and makes each loaf super moist.

Prep time **30 minutes** • Cook time **1 hour** • Yield **2 9-inch (23cm) loaves** • Serving size **1 slice**

3 cups all-purpose flour, plus more for dusting

1 tsp kosher salt

1 tsp baking soda

1 tsp baking powder

1 tbsp ground cinnamon

⊕ 1 tsp ground nutmeg

½ cup butter, melted

½ cup vegetable oil

¾ cup granulated sugar

¾ cup brown sugar

⊕ 3 eggs

⊕ 2 tsp pure vanilla extract (for **Vanilla Extract,** see page 137)

⊕ 2 cups grated zucchini, excess moisture squeezed out

⊕ 1 cup chopped pecans (optional)

1. Preheat the oven to 325°F (190°C). Grease and flour 2 loaf pans.

2. In a large bowl, sift together the flour, salt, baking soda, baking powder, cinnamon, and nutmeg.

3. In the bowl of a stand mixer fitted with the paddle attachment, mix the butter, oil, granulated sugar, and brown sugar. Gradually add the dry ingredients and the eggs, alternating between the two, and mixing fully after each addition. Add the vanilla. Fold in the zucchini and chopped pecans, if using.

4. Divide the batter evenly between the 2 prepared loaf pans. Bake on the center rack for 45 to 60 minutes. The bread is done when a cake tester or toothpick is inserted in a loaf center and comes out clean.

5. Cool on a rack for 20 minutes before inverting out of the bread pan. Cool for an additional 30 minutes before slicing. Serve slathered in softened butter.

NOTES

Be sure to squeeze as much excess moisture as possible from the grated zucchini. Wring it out with your hands or in a cheesecloth.

Wrap tightly with plastic wrap, then aluminum foil, and store in a cool, dry place for up to 1 week.

VARIATION

You can use all granulated sugar or all brown sugar if you do not have both. You can also use walnuts if you prefer them over pecans. Instead of zucchini, try using 2 cups grated carrot.

Blackberry Cobbler

As much as I love pie, I will always pick cobbler first. There is something about that ooey-gooey buttery crust that is only achieved from a cobbler. I have tried cobbler in many different forms over the years, but the kind of crust made from a batter is by far my favorite. It's also the easiest. I love that this recipe is so versatile. You can use any fruit that can stand up to cooking—peaches, apples, blueberries, or even strawberries!

Prep time **20 minutes** • Cook time **30 minutes** • Yield **1 8 × 8-inch (20 × 20cm) cobbler** • Serving size **½ cup**

½ cup butter

1½ cups all-purpose flour

2 tsp baking powder

¼ tsp salt

⊕ 1½ cups milk (whole or 2%)

1 cup granulated sugar, divided

⊕ 2½ cups blackberries (fresh or frozen)

⊕ Zest and juice of 1 lemon

⊕ 1 tsp pure vanilla extract (for **Vanilla Extract,** see page 137)

⊕ 1 tbsp turbinado sugar

⊕ Vanilla ice cream (optional), to serve

1. Preheat the oven to 350°F (175°C). Place the butter in an 8 × 8-inch (20 × 20cm) baking dish, and put it in the oven while the oven preheats to melt the butter.

2. In a medium bowl, mix together the flour, baking powder, salt, milk, and ½ cup sugar. It should resemble pancake batter.

3. In a separate bowl, toss the blackberries with the remaining ½ cup sugar, lemon zest and juice, and vanilla.

4. When the oven has come to temperature and the butter in the baking dish is melted and browned on the edges, pour the batter into the baking dish over the melted butter. Distribute the blackberries evenly on top of the batter, and sprinkle with turbinado sugar. Bake for 25 to 30 minutes until the cobbler is set and bubbly on the edges, and the entire surface is slightly golden brown.

5. Serve warm with vanilla ice cream, if desired.

NOTE
I strongly encourage you to use whole or 2 percent milk. You will not achieve the best texture using low-fat milk or nut milk.

VARIATION
To make an apple pie cobbler, make a double batch of Apple Pie Dip (page 43), chopping the apples into larger chunks. Omit the blackberries, and add large dollops of the Apple Pie Dip to the batter in step 4. Bake as directed.

Chocolate Chip Cookies

I took me a while to master chocolate chip cookies, but I've learned a few tricks to ensure chewy, deeply flavorful cookies every time. Let your butter and eggs come to room temperature (don't cheat by microwaving the butter!); refrigerate the dough overnight; and add a pinch of flaky sea salt just before baking. Follow these tips, and your cookies will be extraordinary.

Prep time **20 minutes + overnight chill** • Cook time **8–10 minutes** • Yield **36 cookies** • Serving size **1 cookie**

2½ cups all-purpose flour

1 tsp baking soda

½ tsp kosher salt

½ cup butter, at room temperature

1 cup packed light brown sugar

1 cup granulated sugar

2 large eggs, at room temperature

1½ tsp pure vanilla extract (for **Vanilla Extract,** see page 137)

2 cups chocolate chips

½ tsp flaky sea salt

1. In a medium bowl, whisk together the flour, baking soda, and salt. Set aside.

2. In the bowl of a stand mixer fitted with the paddle attachment, beat the butter, brown sugar, and granulated sugar on medium-high speed for 3 minutes. Add the eggs, one at a time, and mix until blended. Add the vanilla, and mix until blended.

3. On low speed, add 1 cup of the flour mixture and continue mixing until fully incorporated. Repeat, adding 1 cup of the flour mixture at a time, until all the flour has been added. Turn the mixer to high speed for 5 seconds to pull the dough together. Fold in the chocolate chips. Cover the dough with plastic wrap, and refrigerate overnight or up to 48 hours.

4. Preheat the oven to 350°F (175°C). Line a baking sheet with parchment paper. Remove the dough from the refrigerator and allow to sit for 15 minutes before scooping.

5. Using a medium cookie scoop, drop the dough onto the prepared baking sheet. Be sure to leave about 2 inches (5cm) of space between each cookie. Sprinkle a small pinch of flaky sea salt on each dough ball. Bake for 8 to 10 minutes or until the cookies are lightly browned on top and golden brown on the edges and the bottom. The center of the cookie will still be very soft and appear slightly underbaked. Allow cookies to cool on the baking sheet for 1 minute, and then transfer the cookies to a rack to cool completely. Repeat until all dough has been baked.

NOTE
Unbaked dough can be scooped into balls and frozen on a parchment-lined baking sheet for at least 2 hours. Transfer frozen dough balls to a freezer-safe storage bag. Frozen dough can be stored in the freezer for 2 months. To bake, remove the dough balls from the freezer while the oven preheats. Bake in a 350°F (175°C) oven for 10 to 12 minutes.

Pantry Pie Crust

Pie crust is a staple ingredient. I keep a few disks of pie crust dough in my freezer at all times, so it's that much easier to whip up a pie or quiche. Storing the dough in the freezer until you're ready to use it also helps it come together for maximum flavor and flake.

Prep time **15 minutes + 30 minutes to chill** • Cook time **none** • Yield **2 9-in (23cm) pie crusts** • Serving size **varies**

2½ cups all-purpose flour, plus more for dusting

1 tsp kosher salt

1 tsp granulated sugar (omit for savory applications)

1 cup cold butter, cut into ¼-in (.5cm) cubes

½ cup ice-cold water

1. In a large bowl, whisk together the flour, salt, and sugar, if using. Using a pastry cutter (or 2 forks), cut the cold butter into the flour mixture until the mixture becomes sandy and the butter is broken down into pea-sized pieces.

2. Add 2 tablespoons ice water to the flour mixture and mix gently. Continue adding ice water 1 tablespoon at a time until the flour mixture begins to come together. (You may have ice water leftover.) Stop adding water when the dough holds its shape after being squeezed in your hand.

3. Transfer the dough to a lightly floured surface. Gently shape the dough until it forms a ball, and divide the ball into 2 equal parts. Shape the 2 pieces into 2 disks, each 2 to 3 inches (5–7.5cm) thick, and wrap them with plastic wrap. Refrigerate for at least 30 minutes or up to 3 days before moving on to the next step.

4. Lightly flour a clean, dry work surface. Dust the dough with flour, and use a rolling pin to gently but firmly tap the disk while rotating to create a flatter disk before rolling. It should be about 1 inch (2.5cm) thick at this point. (This helps to maintain its round shape and makes it easier to roll out without cracking.)

5. Roll out the dough, rotating the disk about ¼ inch (.5cm) after each roll. Continue rolling and turning until the crust is about ⅛ inch (3mm) thick. Add a bit more flour to the work surface if needed.

6. To transfer the dough to a pie plate or baking pan, fold the rolled dough in half and then in half again to create a triangle. Place it in your baking dish of choice, and gently unfold it into the pan.

NOTE

Pie crust can be made ahead and stored in the refrigerator for up to 3 days. For later use, place the plastic-wrapped disks in a freezer-safe storage bag and keep them in the freezer for up to 3 months. Remove the dough from the freezer and thaw in the refrigerator for 24 to 48 hours before using.

Bourbon Pecan Pie

Bourbon Pecan Pie is by far the best seller when I make desserts for the holidays. It's my man's favorite and my favorite. This is kind of a no-brainer for me. Pecans are one of my favorite nuts, and bourbon is one of my favorite ingredients. This pie is extra delicious because you can taste the "sting" from the bourbon in the filling.

Prep time **1 hour** • Cook time **45 minutes** • Yield **1 9-inch (23cm) pie** • Serving size **1 slice**

For the crust

1¼ cups all-purpose flour, plus more for dusting

½ tsp granulated sugar

½ tsp kosher salt

½ cup cold butter, cubed

¼ cup ice-cold water

For the filling

3 eggs

1 cup granulated sugar

¼ cup brown sugar, packed

½ tsp kosher salt

1 cup light corn syrup

1 tbsp pure vanilla extract (for **Vanilla Extract,** see page 137)

2 tbsp bourbon

⅓ cup butter, melted

2 cups pecan halves, divided

1. To prepare the crust, in a large bowl, combine the flour, sugar, and salt. Add the butter and mash it into the flour using 2 forks or a pastry blender until the mixture is sandy and the butter is broken down into pea-sized bits. Slowly add the cold water, 1 tablespoon at a time. Stir until the mixture begins to stick together. (You may not end up using all of the water.) The dough should not crumble but should also not be sticky. If the dough does not hold together when squeezed in the palm of your hand, add a bit more water, 1 tablespoon at a time.

2. Knead the dough together a couple of times to form a disk, and wrap with plastic wrap. Refrigerate for at least 45 minutes (up to 3 days if making ahead).

3. While the pie crust chills, prepare the filling. In a large bowl, beat the eggs. Whisk in the granulated sugar, brown sugar, salt, corn syrup, vanilla, bourbon, and butter. Set aside.

4. Preheat the oven to 350°F (175°C).

5. On a lightly floured surface, roll out the pie crust to about 10 inches (25cm). Carefully place the pie crust into a 9-inch (23cm) pie pan. Trim any excess pie crust from around the pie pan and form the crust's edge. Crimp the pie crust with a fork or your fingers.

6. Chop 1 cup pecans, and pour them into the prepared pie crust. Pour in the liquid pie filling. The filling should come just short of the rim of the pie plate. Carefully place the remaining pecan halves on top of the pie filling, going around the entire pie pan until the top of the pie is covered.

7. Bake the pie for 45 to 60 minutes. The center of the pie should be set but jiggle slightly. The pie will continue to firm up as it cools. Allow the pie to cool completely before cutting.

Peach Hand Pies

This recipe combines my favorite fruit, peaches, with my childhood memories of my Grandma Lillie's fried apple pies. Buttery pockets of pie crust are stuffed with warmly spiced, sweet and tangy peaches and then deep fried or baked. I love deep frying them because the crust puffs up a little.

Prep time **20 minutes + 1 hour to freeze** • Cook time **5–7 minutes per pie** • Yield **4 hand pies** • Serving size **1 hand pie**

- 4 large fresh peaches, peeled and diced into 1-in (2.5cm) pieces or 1 (16oz; 450g) bag frozen peach slices, thawed and diced
- ½ cup granulated sugar
- 2 tbsp butter
- ½ tsp ground cinnamon
- ½ tsp freshly ground nutmeg
- ½ tsp kosher salt
- 1 tsp pure vanilla extract (for **Vanilla Extract,** see page 137)
- ½ batch **Pantry Pie Crust** (page 147)

For the glaze
- ½ cup powdered sugar
- 2–3 tbsp milk
- ½ tsp pure vanilla extract (for **Vanilla Extract,** see page 137)

1. To a medium saucepan, add the peaches, sugar, and butter. Place over medium heat. Once the butter is fully melted and the sugar is dissolved, stir in the cinnamon, nutmeg, and salt. Add the vanilla, and reduce the heat to medium-low. Simmer for 12 to 15 minutes or until the peaches are tender. Remove the pot from the heat, and allow the peaches to cool slightly for about 10 minutes.

2. Roll out the pie crust on a lightly floured surface to about 9 inches (23cm). Cut the dough into 8 even wedges. Spoon 1 to 2 tablespoons of filling into the center of 4 wedges. Dip your finger in water and lightly wet the edges of the dough. Gently place the remaining wedges of dough over the wedges with the filling. Use a fork to press around the edges of the pastry, making sure it is fully sealed. Place the pies on a parchment-lined baking sheet, and place in the freezer for 1 hour. (Pies must be frozen before frying; they will burst if not chilled.)

3. To fry the pies, heat the oil in a Dutch oven or heavy-bottomed pot over medium-high heat. (To bake the pies, see Variation.) Use a candy thermometer to regulate the temperature at 350°F (175°C). Carefully place 1 or 2 pies into the hot oil at a time. Cook for 3 to 5 minutes on each side or until golden brown. Transfer to a paper towel–lined plate or a baking sheet fitted with a wire baking rack to drain. Continue frying the pies in batches until they have all been cooked.

4. While the pies are frying, prepare the glaze. In a small bowl, combine the powdered sugar, milk, and vanilla. The glaze should not be lumpy and should drizzle easily. While the pies are cooling, drizzle each pie with a bit of the glaze. Serve warm.

NOTE
Uncooked pies can be frozen in a freezer-safe storage bag and baked or fried when ready.

VARIATION
To bake the pies, brush them with an egg wash and bake in a 400°F (200°C) oven for 20 to 25 minutes or until golden brown.

Lazy Apple Pie

This apple galette is excellent for those who love pie but hate dealing with the perfection of a pie crust. This no-fuss galette makes apple pie making simple while still highlighting tender, tangy apples paired with sweet warm spices.

Prep time **1 hour** • Cook time **30 minutes** • Yield **1 10-inch (25cm) pie** • Serving size **1 slice**

For the crust

1½ cups all-purpose flour, plus more for dusting

½ tsp granulated sugar

½ tsp salt

8 tbsp cold butter, cubed

¼ cup ice-cold water

For the filling

4 tbsp butter

3–4 apples, thinly sliced

1 tbsp ground cinnamon

1 tsp freshly ground nutmeg

1 tsp ground allspice

1 tsp pure vanilla extract (for **Vanilla Extract,** see page 137)

2 tbsp cornstarch

½ cup granulated sugar

1 egg

1 tbsp water

2 tbsp turbinado sugar (optional)

1. To prepare the crust, in a large bowl, combine the flour, sugar, and salt. Add the butter, and mash it into the flour using 2 forks or a pastry blender until the mixture is sandy and the butter is broken down to pea-sized bits. Slowly add the cold water, 1 tablespoon at a time. Stir until the mixture begins to stick together. The dough should not crumble but should also not be sticky. If the dough does not hold together when squeezed in the palm of your hand, add a bit more water, 1 tablespoon at a time. Knead the dough together a couple of times to form a disk, and wrap with plastic wrap. Refrigerate for at least 45 minutes (up to 3 days if making ahead).

2. Preheat the oven to 425°F (220°C). Line a pizza pan or baking sheet with parchment paper.

3. In a small saucepan, melt the butter over medium heat. Continue cooking until the foam subsides and dark brown bits start to form at the bottom of the pan, about 7 minutes. Once the butter has browned, remove from the heat and allow to cool slightly. Set aside.

4. In a large bowl, toss the apple slices with the cinnamon, nutmeg, allspice, vanilla, cornstarch, and granulated sugar.

5. Roll out the dough to about a 12-inch (30.5cm) circle, and gently transfer the dough to the prepared baking sheet. Use a pie pan or 10-inch (25cm) cake pan to make an imprint of a circle in the center of the rolled-out dough. Place the apple filling inside the circle. Fold the edges of the crust up and over the apples, leaving some apples exposed in the center. Pour the browned butter over the apples.

6. In a small bowl, beat the egg with the water. Using a pastry brush, brush the exterior of the crust with egg wash, and sprinkle with turbinado sugar, if using. Bake for 30 minutes or until golden brown. Let sit for 10 minutes before slicing.

VARIATION

This galette can also be made with fresh pears or fresh or frozen blueberries. If using blueberries, omit the spices and replace them with the zest and juice of 1 lemon.

Lillie's Sweet Potato Pie Bars

There is a secret club for Black women that requires a special initiation. It's called the Sweet Potato Pie Club. In order to gain membership, you must make the perfect sweet potato pie filling with just the right amount of sugar and warm spices. I strongly believe the founder of that club was my Grandma Lillie. I channel her every time I make sweet potato pie, and I officially became a member the first time I got it right. I took it a step further and created this bar with perfectly spiced filling and a decadent, cookie-like crust in her honor.

Prep time **1 hour** • Cook time **1 hour 20 minutes** • Yield **9 bars** • Serving size **1 bar**

For the crust
½ cup butter, softened
½ cup granulated sugar
1 cup all-purpose flour
¼ tsp kosher salt

For the filling
3 large sweet potatoes
½ cup butter, softened
½ cup granulated sugar
¾ cup all-purpose flour
1 tbsp ground cinnamon
⊕ 1 tsp freshly ground nutmeg
⊕ 1 tsp ground allspice
½ tsp kosher salt
⊕ 3 eggs
⊕ 1 cup heavy cream
⊕ 1 tsp pure vanilla extract
(for **Vanilla Extract,** see page 137)

1. To make the crust, in the bowl of a stand mixer fitted with the paddle attachment, cream together the butter and the sugar. The mixture should be pale yellow. Slowly add the flour and mix until fully incorporated. Mix in the salt. The mixture should be crumbly but hold together when gently squeezed on the palm of your hand.

2. Transfer the dough to a parchment-lined 8 × 8-inch (20 × 20cm) metal baking dish. Using floured hands, press the dough into the baking dish. Chill for at least 1 hour or up to overnight.

3. Preheat the oven to 350°F (175°C). Bake the crust for 20 to 25 minutes until lightly brown. Set aside to cool.

4. To make the filling, place the whole, unpeeled sweet potatoes into a large pot and add water to cover. Bring to a boil over high heat, and boil for 20 minutes or until fork-tender. Remove the pot from the heat and drain the water. Allow the potatoes to cool for about 15 minutes, and then carefully remove the peel from each potato.

5. To the bowl of a stand mixer, add the sweet potatoes. Using the whisk attachment, place the mixer on medium-low speed. Add the butter, sugar, flour, cinnamon, nutmeg, and allspice. Mix until combined. Add the eggs one at a time, ensuring each egg is thoroughly mixed in before adding another. Slowly mix in the cream and vanilla. Turn off the mixer as soon as both are fully incorporated.

6. Pour the sweet potato mixture into the cooled crust. Bake for 45 minutes or until the center is no longer jiggly. Let cool completely before cutting into 12 bars.

NOTES

Consider adding ½ teaspoon ground ginger to the filling if you have it.

Bars can be served reheated to warm or at room temperature. To store, refrigerate in an airtight container.

Judy's Rice Pudding

My Grandma Judy made the best rice pudding. Even though it was made with humble ingredients, it tasted like it came out of a five-star restaurant. She added just the right amount of warm spices and sugar to make each bite comforting and delicious. Her rice pudding is baked in the oven, which makes it creamy, custardy, and luxurious.

Prep time **15 minutes** • Cook time **1 hour 30 minutes** • Yield **6 cups** • Serving size **½ cup**

3 cups water

1½ cups long-grain white rice, rinsed

1½ tsp kosher salt, divided

4 tbsp butter, divided

⊕ 2 eggs

⊕ 1 cup whole milk

⊕ 1½ cups heavy cream

1 cup granulated sugar

1 tsp ground cinnamon

⊕ ½ tsp ground nutmeg

⊕ 1 tsp pure vanilla extract (for **Vanilla Extract,** see page 137)

1. In a medium pot, bring the water to boil over high heat. Once boiling, stir in the rinsed rice and 1 teaspoon salt. Cover the pot with a lid, and reduce the heat to low. Cook for 15 to 20 minutes or until most of the liquid has been absorbed. Remove the lid, and fluff the rice with a fork. Spread the cooked rice evenly on a baking sheet. Cover with plastic wrap and allow to cool. After 15 minutes, place the baking sheet in the refrigerator for 1 hour or up to overnight.

2. Preheat the oven to 350°F (175°C). Grease an 8 × 8-inch (20 × 20cm) glass baking dish with 1 tablespoon butter. Melt the remaining 3 tablespoons butter, and set aside.

3. In a medium bowl, whisk together the eggs, milk, and heavy cream. Continue whisking for 2 to 3 minutes until the eggs are fully incorporated with no streaks of egg yolk remaining. The mixture should be slightly foamy and resemble pale orange juice. Whisk in the sugar. Add the melted butter, cinnamon, nutmeg, vanilla, and the remaining ½ teaspoon salt. Whisk until the spices are evenly distributed throughout the mixture and the sugar is dissolved.

4. Use your hands to crumble up the chilled rice into the bowl of the custard mixture. Stir until all of the rice is coated. Pour the mixture into the prepared baking dish, and bake for 50 to 60 minutes. The pudding is done when the edges are firm and the middle is slightly jiggly. Let the pudding sit for 15 minutes before serving. Serve warm or cold.

NOTES

This recipe is a perfect way to use up leftover cooked rice. It can also be made with brown rice. For brown rice, cook according to the package instructions, and cool as directed before continuing to step 2.

Rice pudding is traditionally made with raisins, but I don't like raisins. If you are not a member of the "Raisins Are Gross Club," feel free to toss in ½ cup raisins when you add the rice to the custard mixture in step 4.

Crème Brûlée

With its crackling crust of browned sugar, crème brûlée looks and sounds fancy, but it's actually simple to make. The creamy vanilla custard requires just a few ingredients, and it can easily be prepared ahead, making it a go-to dinner party dessert.

Prep time **15 minutes + 4 hours to chill** • Cook time **45 minutes** • Yield **6 6oz (175ml) ramekins** • Serving size **1 ramekin**

⊕ 4 cups heavy cream

⊕ 2 tsp pure vanilla extract (for **Vanilla Extract,** see page 137)

⊕ 6 egg yolks

½ tsp kosher salt

1 cup granulated sugar, divided

1. Preheat the oven to 325°F (160°C). In a medium saucepan, heat the heavy cream and vanilla over medium heat. Do not allow the mixture to come to a boil. It should be hot and slightly steamy.

2. Meanwhile, in a medium bowl, vigorously whisk the egg yolks with the salt and ½ cup sugar.

3. Remove the hot cream from the heat. Use a ladle to add about ½ cup of the hot cream to the egg mixture, whisking as you add it. Go slowly so the hot cream does not scramble the eggs. Repeat this step twice, and then slowly add the contents of the bowl to the saucepan while whisking to combine. Set aside.

4. Prepare a bain-marie (hot water bath). In a kettle or saucepan, bring 4 cups water to a boil. Pour the boiling water into a roasting pan; the water should come about halfway up the sides of the pan.

5. Carefully ladle the egg mixture into six 6-ounce (175ml) ramekins, and place them in the roasting pan with the water. Carefully place the roasting pan in the oven, and bake for 30 to 45 minutes. The custard with be slightly jiggly in the middle but set on the edges.

6. Remove the ramekins from the roasting pan and allow them to cool to room temperature. Cover each ramekin with plastic wrap and refrigerate for at least 4 hours or up to 1 week.

7. Remove the ramekins from the refrigerator and let them sit at room temperature for 30 minutes. Remove the plastic wrap, and spread about 1 tablespoon sugar on top of each custard. Use a kitchen torch to melt the sugar while slowly turning the ramekin to ensure the sugar is browning evenly. Let sit for 5 minutes before serving.

NOTES

If you don't have a blow torch, brown the sugar under the broiler. Place the ramekins on a baking sheet, and put them on the top rack of the oven. Broil on high for 1 to 3 minutes. Check every minute to ensure the sugar does not burn.

Do not torch the sugar until you are ready to serve.

Index

T–U–V

W–X–Y–Z

Acknowledgments

I would not understand the unique gift food can represent if it weren't for the Culinary Institute of My Parents and Grandparents. They instilled a legacy of memories and skill that make it possible to do what I do. Grandma Lillie, I think about you every single day. I feel you in the kitchen with me when making a sweet potato pie or fried corn. I hope I am half as good a cook as you were.

My parents created an environment that was limitless. As long as I got an education and worked hard, I could do anything I wanted to do. Thank you, Mom and Dad, for supporting me and investing in me when I decided to make a wild and crazy career change at 35 years old. You cheered me on through every step of my corporate career, and you cheer me on just as loudly now. I appreciate you both more than you know.

Johntay, you are the softened Kerrygold butter and apple jelly to my warm and fluffy biscuit. I am overwhelmed with how well you love me on a regular basis. You believe in me when I don't believe in myself. Thank you for being the safest place for me to fall and the softest place for me to land. I love you.

To my tribe: Jodi, Susanna, Tricia, and Alicia—thank you for keeping me humble, celebrating my wins, and being my village.

To my team: my creative director, Rebecca Bratz; kitchen assistant, Jonelle Utt; creative coach, Chitra Panjabi; recipe tester, Diamond Alexander; literary agent, Leigh Eisenman; and editor, Ann Barton—*Staples* +5 wouldn't exist without you. Holy crap, I wrote a cookbook!

Beyoncé, Tobe Nwigwe, and the original cast of *Hamilton*— thank you for helping me rock out in my kitchen daily. I danced to you while writing every single recipe.

Lastly, thank you to every single person who has encouraged me, devoured my food, connected with me on the interwebs, watched me on TV, or made an impact on my life in any other way. You constantly remind me why cooking and connection are so important. I am forever grateful.

ABOUT THE AUTHOR

Tanorria Askew is the owner of Tanorria's Table, a personal chef company based in Indianapolis, Indiana. Tanorria was born in Chattanooga, Tennessee, and her cooking roots are based on Southern family tradition. In 2016, Tanorria ended her 15-year career in banking and learning and development to pursue her dream of empowering people through food. She was crowned fourth best cook in America on *MasterChef* Season 7, hosted by Gordon Ramsay.

Tanorria continues to build her business through virtual cooking classes, dinner parties, and racial justice activism. You can find her dancing to Beyoncé in her flour-covered kitchen or relaxing with her partner and their three dogs.